WRITING
from the
SOURCE

WRITING
from the
SOURCE

Techniques for
rescripting your life

ALLISON PRICE

Thorsons
An Imprint of HarperCollins*Publishers*

Thorsons
An Imprint of HarperCollins*Publishers*
77–85 Fulham Palace Road,
Hammersmith, London W6 8JB

First published 1999
1   3   5   7   9   10   8   6   4   2

© 1999 Allison Price

Allison Price asserts the moral right to
be identified as the author of this work

A catalogue record for this book
is available from the British Library

ISBN 0 7225 3683 6

Printed and bound in Great Britain by
Creative Print and Design (Wales)

CONTENTS

ACKNOWLEDGEMENTS

Having had the temerity to write a book of this kind, one which dares to offer suggestions to others on how to live their lives, I think it behoves me to make it very clear that almost every technique and insight appearing in these pages came to me through someone else's knowledge or experience. Certainly I owe an enormous debt to the authors whose thoughts are quoted so lavishly throughout. There would scarcely be a book at all without them.

But there are others, closer to home, to whom I must also give my deepest appreciation. To Dr Glen Dey, who taught me what I know about this uneasy business of counselling; to each one of my clients through the years who shared their lives and helped me find my way; to Anita Skeen, that Pied Piper, who has taught so many of us the power of the pen and the journal; and to Vicky Stamp, Nancy Smith and Linda Talbott, whose friendship and laughter and wisdom turned my first attempts at journalling into an addiction – to all of you, inestimable thanks.

I can never stop being grateful to my terrific agent (and now my friend), Sugra Zaman, who salvaged this book from her slush pile and believed in it enough to see it through to the end. You know what your faith and patience have meant to me.

And the last shall be first: Mother, Adam, Murray and Kate. Throughout it was your interest and encouragement which kept me going. But in your case, Briarly Kate, it's quite simple. Without you, I wouldn't, I couldn't have written it at all.

CHAPTER 1

INTRODUCTION

*People often say that this or that person has not
yet found himself. But the self is not something
one finds, it is something one creates.*

THOMAS SZASZ

Your first thought, looking at the title of this book, might
well have been, 'The *source*? What *source*? What in the
world does that mean?' Well, it's easy enough to define,
but it's often much more difficult to find. Because the source is
you – your unique, authentic self, that true centre which, by the
time you are old enough to be interested in reading a book like
this, may have become so overlaid by everyone else's expectations,
values and definitions that you yourself no longer feel much confidence about who exactly that 'you' is: what it is that *you* feel,
what *you* believe. We are often advised to trust our instincts. And
this is great advice, if we can only be sure that our instincts speak
to us from a still, uncluttered centre of truth within us. But for
most of us, that core has been silenced by the noises of our lives.
My job, in the pages of this book, is to share with you some techniques for clearing out much of that clutter – techniques which

I hope will help you to rediscover that honest core of self which may have been buried for too much of your life.

Take a moment to read again the quote from Thomas Szasz at the beginning of the chapter and consider how it might apply to you. What 'self' have you created thus far? Does it suit you? Does it suit the people in your life who mean the most to you? Is your self a comfortable fit for you? Does the self you present to the world reflect the truth of what you believe yourself to be? If, as you think through all of the implications of Szasz's observation and your responses to it, you are aware that your 'creation' is not entirely what you intended, then get ready to do some work. I might just as easily have called this book *Writing Your Life* because that's what this book is about: exercises for examining the life you've created thus far – and then further exercises for rewriting the script of that life so that it reflects your needs, your values, your truest self.

A quick caveat here. I am a counsellor. That is both my training and my focus. And although I promise to avoid most of the jargon of my trade, there is one word I cannot duck with euphemisms. That word is 'neurotic'.

I'm complex, you're eccentric, he's nuts. Those are three different labels which all mean exactly the same thing – the only difference is who is doing the labelling. Because the truth is, to be normal is to be neurotic. More simply still, *to be neurotic is to be human*. Strip away all the psycho-babble, the jargon, the labels and grab on to this – Fritz Perls' splendidly elegant definition of neurosis: 'the inability to see the obvious'. So, at least for the purposes of this book, I will use that word as a shorthand for confused, conflicted, bewildered, unsure, self-deluding, blocked, mixed-up … . You get the idea. The list of adjectives could go on for pages, but they would all mean the same thing. The shorthand is 'neurotic'. The underlying truth is 'human'. No more, no less.

So here are two truths you might want to reflect on if it makes you a little skittish to think the word 'neurotic' might ever apply to you: Dev Winnicott's observation that 'we are poor indeed if we are only sane', and another by the great Dr. Szasz, 'The difference between normal and abnormal is not what you do but how much you do it.'

Neither in my counselling nor in my personal life have I ever known anyone, including myself, who has not at some time become so enmeshed in a relationship or a situation that they can no longer see the truth of it, or find a way out of it. And if such a completely detached observer of life did exist, that is a neurosis in itself, and probably a more difficult one to break through than all the others. And what an arid way it would be to live.

So this book is for us – for all the *normal* neurotics out there. We are people who live basically happy, productive lives, who have an acceptable number of friends, have work (paid or otherwise) which is more or less satisfying, possibly have children and partners. We are certainly *not* nuts – at least, not obviously and not most of the time. But whether our 'problem' is a relationship that never quite fails but certainly hasn't succeeded, an issue about ourselves that nags at us but never improves, or an uneasy, unnecessary numbness as we live what the world would consider successful lives, we are neurotic. We are unable to see our obvious. Perhaps the most frightening example of this (and, admittedly, at the extreme edge of the normal range) is the anorexic – literally, obviously, starving to death but still convinced that she, and occasionally he, is too fat.

And if it is true that to be human is to be – at least to some degree – neurotic, then it is obviously also true that there is no cure for it. But there *are* a number of very helpful techniques which we can use to help us see more deeply, more clearly into those areas of our lives which are not working for us.

I use the plural here because, though I am a trained counsellor and have practised as such for a number of years, I learned from my very first client that the only thing that generally differentiated us – leaving aside the financial arrangements – was that she did most of the talking, and I sat in the counsellor's chair. Which, if you grant me the courtesy of assuming that I mean that and wasn't just being disingenuous, leads to the obvious question, 'Why pay a counsellor, then, if they are as screwed up as I am and all they do is listen?' There are, of course, a number of answers to that – one of which is that you may not need to at all. A good friend can sometimes be every bit as helpful as a good counsellor. They can listen without judging, they can hear your concerns without trying to tell you what you should do about them, and they can help you become aware of your patterns of thoughts and actions.

But the problem is, you can't count on it. For one thing, your perceptions are cloudy (or you wouldn't be asking for help in the first place), so you may not choose the ideal confidant. For another, a good friend cannot help but have their own agenda, well-intentioned or not. Whether they are hindered by the loving wish to make you feel better or, perhaps, the unconsciously unloving one of settling an old score, they can rarely be objective enough to help you take the vital next step – deciding just what you're getting out of holding on to your neurosis – and how to let go of it. If you *do* have a friend who fits these criteria, cancel your therapist's appointment, return this book to the shop for a refund, and call that friend over for a cup of coffee and a long talk.

Know this: the secret is, there is no secret! Psychologists do not know one thing more about being human than you do. Nor are there any books which have the answers, because there are no answers. There are as many ways of being human as there are human beings in the world and each way is just as good as the next, *so long as it does not cause unnecessary pain – either to yourself or to others.* (On the other hand, good literature at least asks the right questions and offers powerful insights to the human experience, so you'll find more literature quoted in these pages than therapeutic theory.)

But, if you are courageous enough to tell yourself the truth, and open enough to hear that truth you have told, you are completely capable of transcending the most limiting of your own normal hang-ups and problems. And those abilities can be called into play throughout your life, whenever the need arises.

It was Thomas Szasz who said, 'People go into therapy not to get better but to improve their neurosis.' The fact is, most of us actually have no intention of changing – we want to go on doing exactly what we have been doing, except that we would like to make those behaviours work for us for a change. Fair enough. But the important thing to remember here is that you got as far as buying this book precisely because some of these behaviours weren't working for you any more. This difficulty is compounded by this second fact – most of us derive considerable satisfaction from those very aspects which other people consider the craziest things about us. We'll look at that, too.

Change is hard. Because change, even for the better, always involves some psychological loss. It demands that we learn to let go of a lifetime's worth of habits of seeing, habits of being – and it demands the acceptance that *we may have been wrong*. But assuming that you have, however grudgingly, accepted that some small alteration might be beneficial, the trick then becomes how to begin to see your 'obvious' so that a shift of perception and behaviour might occur. That's what this book is about.

CHAPTER 2

FINDING MY WAY

In a dark time, the eye begins to see.
ROETHKE

I saw my very first client as part of my practical work in my final year of training. Sometimes I still wake up sweating with the memory. There I was, wearing the professional (yet friendly and reassuring) outfit that had only taken me five weeks to choose, my tape recorder ready to be switched on (for the benefit of my supervisor, who would monitor all sessions through those recordings and later go through them with me), full of intellectual theories about 'the human condition' and how to improve it. I sat there that day, nervous, but fully prepared to offer myself as a living repository of all insight and compassion and wisdom.

The woman who entered the room, whom I'll call Mona, could have posed for a portrait entitled *Desolation*. Lank hair, eyes bleak, shoulders hunched, head drooping, she sagged listlessly in her chair and, after only the barest of preliminaries, said, in a voice so dull and lifeless that I had to strain to hear her, 'Well, I guess I'd better tell you right off. I'm an alcoholic and I killed my baby.'

Writing this now, everything returns to me: my fading smile, the physical sensation of blood draining from my face, an overwhelming dizziness and the terror that I was going to pass out cold on the spot. Above all, my own struggle not to blurt out, 'Wait! There's been some dreadful mistake. I'm not a *real* counsellor! I have no idea how to deal with this and I'm desperately sorry, but I have to go home now.'

I don't know what I said in reply to Mona's statement. (Please God don't let it have been that therapist's standby 'And how do you feel about that?'!) I do know that it was, literally, long minutes before the blackness cleared a bit and my faintness eased enough for me to limp along with at least some minimal participation. *Days* later the hour finally ended, both of us shaky but still game for another session the next week – Mona because she was in much too much pain to be aware of my absolute inadequacy, and I because I had gone too far down the path of my training to know how to back out at that late stage. But how I wanted to!

It was many years before I appreciated that virtually everything I now know about counselling I was to learn in that year which Mona and I spent together. All my experiences with other clients since have only confirmed or intensified what Mona and Dr. Glen Dey, my splendid supervisor, taught me during that remarkable time.

Before I go any further, I want to say that Mona is now happily married, the mother of three children, the manager of her own thriving small business, and has been alcohol-free for nearly 20 years. And all of that is true because of Mona's need – which I believe to be a basic human need that we all share – to make sense of pain, to move beyond it, and to live as fully as our courage and determination allow. Absolutely *not* because of me.

Mona improved her life and the circumstances of it because the human spirit is so wonderfully unquenchable. I need to make clear too that it was Mona who did the work. Certainly I was too new and inexperienced to offer much beyond a non-judging ear. But I did care and, with Dr. Dey's counsel and Mona's growing determination, that caring – and the awareness that I was *on her side* – gave her the safe space she needed to begin to heal.

That basic resiliency of the human spirit was my first great lesson – and the one that has given me the temerity to believe that a book like this can be useful. Because you must care about yourself (or you wouldn't be reading this) and you are, surely, on your own side. My hope is that the work you will do throughout these chapters will provide your own safe space for healing.

'I guess I'd better tell you right off. I'm an alcoholic and I killed my baby.' Those first, terrifying words of Mona hold a key to the most important psychological truth you will ever have to accept to be able to free yourself from your own conflicts. As Cardinal Newman said, '*We can believe what we choose. We are answerable for what we choose to believe.*' Until you have drawn your last breath, you have it within your power to alter whatever choices of belief you may have made in the past. You will not be able to transcend your neurosis if you do not accept this reality: *change is a choice. You have the power to change what you believe to be true about yourself.*

It is true that that first day in my office Mona was beginning the fight against her addiction to alcohol. What was *not* true was that she had killed her baby – though that was the 'fact' that she had decided to tell herself, due to her self-loathing. She believed it to be at least morally true, and her belief was destroying her. Mona's baby was a 'cot death' victim, or Sudden Infant Death Syndrome. Like all SIDS deaths, it was tragic and devastating and, because doctors still find such deaths rather inexplicable, harder to accept than if the exact causes had been understood. But Mona's despair at the shape of her life had not begun with her child's death. Rather, it was *because* of her despair and self-contempt that, when her little girl did die a natural death, Mona herself labelled the experience in that most punishing and self-destructive way.

For a number of reasons, Mona had decided quite young that she had no value, that everything she tried turned to failure and, perhaps most damaging of all, that she *deserved* whatever bad things happened to her. Mona had a tremendous task ahead of her. First, she had to learn *why* she had decided to view herself so negatively. Most of all, she had to learn to recast the image that she had created of herself and fashion another to put in its place.

I realize there is a good chance that you may have read Mona's story and thought, 'Well, that's heartbreaking, of course. But what does it have to do with me? I thought this book was for average people with *normal* neuroses.' Certainly I hope your life has not contained such dramatic or destructive examples of self-labelling. But your job is still identical to the one Mona faced – the only difference is of degree. Even for you, it is axiomatic that you will have chosen to name many of your characteristics and experiences in ways which are hurtful to you and almost certainly hurtful to those you love. The odds are pretty good too that, as in Mona's case, many of those labels will fall very short of the truth.

As elementary as it sounds, I have come to believe that most self-destructive attitudes and behaviours are the result of simple bad habits – habits of response, of focus, of expectation, of belief, of conduct. And as Thomas à Kempis wrote, 'Habit is overcome by habit.' So you are going to have to identify the messages you have got into the habit of giving yourself about yourself and your life. That done, you must examine and question those messages. Then will come your greatest challenge: the relabelling of those messages so that you can begin to build new, positive habits to take their place. Charles Reade said, 'Sow an act and you reap a habit. Sow a character and you reap a destiny.'

I promise you, if Mona could do it, so can you.

CHAPTER 3

CATCHING
THE HARE

As long as you are trying to be something other than what you actually are, your mind wears itself out. But if you can say, 'This is what I am. It is fact that I am going to investigate, understand', then you can go beyond.

KRISHNAMURTI

As Mrs. Beeton wrote considering the preparation of hare in her famous Victorian cookery book, 'First you catch your hare ... .'

Here the hare in question is, of course, yourself, and catching it is going to be just as full of adventure – and as difficult – as if it were an actual hare you were after. Assuming we have no axe to grind, most of us usually do rather well at understanding people whom we are not too closely involved with: we don't get bogged down by their details. Where we *ourselves* are concerned, however, it is a very different matter. We tend not to be able to get beyond our details: the desire to nurse our grievances, the pleasures of wallowing in self-pity, the need to justify our behaviours, the endless replay of ' "I said" and then "he said ..." '.

So the job becomes how to see past your particulars to get to your general. Learning to 'see the obvious' is often simply a case of being able to see the forest, not just the trees. And here comes the part that most people resist like crazy.

Though I hope you will find a number of helpful techniques in this book, I am going to start with the most demanding and the most useful. You are going to have to do a *lot* of writing – that's all there is to it. Pen and paper, typewriter, computer, your finger dipped in your own blood (and sometimes it will feel like that!), it doesn't matter. It must be done – there's really no help for it. I'll remind you again that people go to counsellors – and pay them a great deal of money – not to be given advice, not just to be listened to, but to be heard – and even more importantly, to learn how to hear for themselves. As your own counsellor, your job is the same – to surprise yourself into an insight to which your old habits of expectation, beliefs, etc. have blinded you. And I know no way of doing it for yourself except by writing.

Worse still, you're going to have to value – and discipline – yourself enough to do this nearly every day for months, perhaps longer. As I write this, I can almost guarantee one of two reactions:

- an overzealous surge of enthusiasm which is bound to fizzle out before the week is over, or, and even more likely,
- an impatient shrug as you mutter to yourself, 'Oh well, that's probably true in general, and I'll do it when I have the time. But when I don't, I'll just read the exercises and do them in my head.'

It can't be done. This hare we're after is as elusive and cunning as the devil – and most of the time it's hidden effectively among the trees which we can't see beyond.

You simply *must* have a large enough collection of experiences, musings, dreams, desires, sorrows, concerns, pleasures – the incidents of your life – for a pattern to begin to emerge so that you can examine what that pattern tells you about yourself. And if you haven't written these thoughts down, they will not be available to you. All of us remember highly selectively at best, so you cannot count on memory alone to help you. More than that, every writer will tell you that something happens during the act of writing itself which seems to tap into an area of consciousness that is not normally available to us. Often, in fact, the words will create, or liberate, a thought you had not even realized you had. Then, as you read it over later, even if only from the distance of a few days, you will be much more able to consider what that thought or event means to you. Says to you.

Many people, in the attempt to do *anything* to avoid the effort of putting words on paper, will think they've licked the problem by doing their 'writing' into a tape recorder. I must tell you, this does not work. Even aside from the fact that listening to your own voice will unnerve you to such an extent that you won't be able to hear what you are telling yourself, it takes much longer to listen than to read – and you're much more easily distracted while doing so. It is *essential* to the usefulness of these exercises that you are able to refer to them readily and often.

This process of making your 'obvious' apparent may start after only a few days of keeping your diary – and the more you contribute to it, the faster and the deeper your progress will be. If you write as honestly as you are able, and read it later with the same openness to what you have written, insight is unavoidable. Eventually you will have one of those 'Aha!' experiences that psychologists are so fond of, and you will find yourself saying something like, 'Ahhh. I see. That time was with the kids at the supermarket and that time was in a meeting at the office, but it was really the same issue that made me angry [or happy or sad, whatever] – only the details were different.' The first time that happens, you have your hare by the tail – and though there is obviously plenty of hard, messy work ahead, you're on your way. In fact, if you have the courage and the *need* to make some shift in perception and/or approach, at this point nothing will deflect you.

A quick psychological insight here may be encouraging. Counsellors who specialize in relationship dynamics will tell you that if one member of a group (familial, business, social, whatever) changes, all the other members will necessarily change as well, because there has been a break in the pattern. Now at first this may be unnerving for everyone concerned, but if your problem is a 'group' problem, hang in there, keep doing what is necessary for you to do and, again as they say in this field, trust the process.

My task in these pages is to share some of the techniques and insights towards change which have been useful for me as a counsellor. The work, however, is yours. If you do it, you may be able to save yourself a great deal of time and money in a therapist's room. But make no mistake – the cost (at least emotionally) will still be high. This is difficult and sometimes painful work. It is also absorbing, often great fun, and can be enormously rewarding. So tell yourself your first truth: you are worth 30 minutes a day – longer if you can, when you can.

Before I begin with the first suggested exercises (which I trust will lead eventually to you developing your own), I must make clear my own very strong and very personal bias in this whole matter of individual analysis. I have no interest in encouraging anyone to use psychological insights as tools for assigning blame, avoiding personal responsibility or perfecting new skills to define themselves as victims. All lives are personal stories – some will be more obviously tragic, some more clearly comic. Your job is to decide what kind of story yours has been *up till now*, and then to decide how you plan to go about shaping it in the future.

William James said 'men can alter their lives by altering their attitudes'. Since we cannot control all the circumstances of our lives, it behoves us to learn to recognize the ways we contribute to those circumstances. And just as important, we need to learn that we do have the power to alter our attitudes to the events of our lives. You alone are the consumer of your life. You are also the sole source for determining the direction that life will take. Your task now is to compose your life and your growth in ways that will enhance your satisfaction with them – and the satisfaction of those you love.

CHAPTER 4

GETTING STARTED

What you have become is the price you paid to
get what you used to want.
MIGNON McLAUGHLIN

Feelings are facts – they are not negotiable. Which is not to say that they are immutable. Time, experience and insight may alter the 'facts' you feel but, for now, what you believe about your life has become the truth of your life for you. No matter that your family, your friends, even the rest of the world could argue, rightly, the factual inaccuracy of events as you remember them. For you at least, those memories have become the truth. As Shirley Hazzard has written, 'Sometimes, surely, truth is closer to imagination – or to intelligence, to love – than to fact? To be accurate is not to be right.'

The purpose of the exercises contained in this chapter is two-fold. First, they are a sort of limbering-up: to ease you into learning to experiment with ways of creating experiences on paper which can help you see beyond your obvious to whatever emotional realities are hidden from you. Second, they offer a way for you to begin to examine the assumptions on which you habitually act:

assumptions about yourself, your place in the world, even the world in general. Such assumptions will determine how you label every experience of your life. But if you are not aware of them, you are unable to challenge them.

Your first step, then, into your own self-analysis, is to look over the list of topics I've suggested below, and select one to write about. For three weeks do this *every* day, choosing, of course, a new topic each time. Promise yourself at least 30 minutes a session. If you can give even longer, the benefits to you will be that much greater. Write whatever the topic suggests to you: the only requirement is that you do not edit your thoughts and that you promise complete honesty in what you write.

When you have finished, read your work over quickly, just to make sure it will be legible to you in the future. Do not subtract anything! Add to it if you have time and feel the need, but take *nothing* out. Then put it in a safe place you have chosen for it and don't look at it again for at least three weeks.

According to Socrates, 'The unexamined life is not worth living.' Well, whether you are about to take your first or your thousandth step into this examination of your life, it is bound to be an enthralling journey and I hope you enjoy it.

SOME GENERAL SUGGESTIONS BEFORE YOU BEGIN

1. Carry a notebook, a couple of index cards, whatever, *something* to make notes on as you go through your day. Then if you're stuck waiting at the dentist's, or the car wash, or on a train – wherever – take a moment to jot down anything that

occurs to you of interest (about yourself, your reactions, your emotions), which you might want to elaborate on when you have the time. Then later, when you do have the time, *do it.*

2. Give yourself a break. This is not a literacy test, nor an exam to be graded. Spelling, punctuation, none of that matters. You are your own detective here, chasing down clues to yourself. If you can read your work, you've done well enough.

3. Keep all of your work together in one place. If it pleases you to write everything in matching – or contrasting – brocaded notebooks, by all means do so. If your style is more of the yellow legal-pad variety, do that instead. If you do your best thinking at the computer, print out copies of your work and keep those copies all together in a folder (as opposed to a file in your machine). You *must* be able to see the patterns emerge and it is infinitely easier to do this with the actual papers in your hands, leaf-throughable, than it is switching from file to file on your computer screen.

4. Keep your work some place that only you have access to – under lock and key, if that's the only way to ensure complete privacy. There are two reasons for this. First, you must be able to be as honest as you have it within you to be, however shameful, humiliating or unacceptable your thoughts and actions may appear to you, or however hurtful to (or about) others they are. And second, these diaries are not weapons to be left around 'inadvertently' to tease or punish whoever might read them. Now reread that last sentence.

5. Some days it will seem that you truly don't have a minute to yourself. Don't use this as an excuse for not writing at all

(because once you stop, even briefly, it is too easy never to start again – at which point you have one more broken promise to reprove yourself with). When those days do come, force yourself to write down at least 10 quick trigger words with the mental promise that the *next day* you will return to those words and develop whatever thoughts they carry with them. Then keep your promise.

6. Do not fall into the journalist's trap of believing that the only events worth reporting are the bad or sad ones. You are attempting to gain a picture of the entire scope of your life. Record your happy times, the times you laugh, with at least as much dedication as you give to the more serious ones.

7. I don't want to encourage schizophrenia here, but it sometimes helps to write about yourself in the third person. Since the major purpose of keeping these diaries is to be able to get enough emotional distance from your thoughts and feelings to see the larger picture more clearly, occasionally approach your writing as if you were only one character in a novel. When you do this, throw in lots of adverbs; for example, 'I said, sadly', or 'he said, maliciously', etc. The adverbs or adjectives you choose can be terrific clues to recognizing your true agenda, and your perception of the agenda of the others involved in the scenario. Remember, what you are after is *your* truth: accuracy as such is not required, emotional honesty is.

8. Give yourself the gift of elaboration. Whatever topic you choose each time, let your mind roam and, staying with the subject you have chosen, use all the colours on your palette.

Are other people a part of the story you're telling yourself? Describe them and examine what they meant to you during the situation you're writing about. Is place important? Weather? Smell? Sight? Touch? Age? Consider all these aspects, and any others that occur to you, and incorporate them as fully as you are able. If, as you write, you find yourself surprised by what you are saying or feeling, *absolutely* include that fact and the nature of it into your work.

9. The time frame I suggest for these writings is arbitrary and, at the very most, a mild suggestion. If you want to work at these jottings (or any others in the book) for a week – or weeks – of course that's up to you. There is nothing psychologically magic about 'an exercise a day – 30 minutes minimum'. That may seem like an almost insulting statement of the obvious, but as a 'normal neurotic', the odds are that you will tend to be either a compulsive rule-follower or a compulsive rule-breaker, and I want you to recognize that any 'rules' you find in these pages are of your own devising. After all, you didn't develop your patterns of thought overnight, and it is very unlikely that you'll suddenly be able to see your obvious one morning simply because of an entry you wrote the day before. All of these writings are devised to help you identify the antecedents for the attitudes and behaviours which are limiting you now.

4. Write in as much detail as you can about two people (besides your parents) you've learned from. What did you learn? Did you learn it through example? Words? Attitudes? Actions? Thoughts? Approach to life? What was it about these people that engaged you? Was what you learned a blessing or a curse? Do you still believe that lesson? Do you want to?

5. Hofmannsthal wrote, 'Where is your Self to be found? Always in the deepest enchantment that you have experienced.' Identify, remember and explore your 'deepest enchantment'. Does your life currently include such experiences? If not, why not? Could it? If those exact experiences are no longer available to you, can you devise others which *are* possible in your life now and could fulfil the same needs?

6. 'If you do not hope, you will not find what is beyond your hopes', said St Clement of Alexandria. Begin your page with the words, 'I hope ...' and write on this subject as completely as you can.

7. Remember the book entitled *Everything You Ever Wanted to Know About Sex but Were Afraid to Ask*? Write: 'As a sexual partner, I am ... ', 'As a sexual partner, I am not ... ', 'In a sexual partner, I would like ... ', and, finally, 'In my life, sex is ... '.

8. Think about the job (paid or otherwise) in your life which gave you the greatest satisfaction. Can you identify what it was about it that pleased and engaged you? Is it work you are still doing? Does it still suit you? If not, what has changed — you or the work? If you now do other work, why did you make the change? Are you glad that you did?

9. 'Watch what people are cynical about and you can often discover what they lack.' Henry Emerson Fosdick. Think for a bit about what you are cynical about. Does Fosdick's statement fit for you? Write about what lack your cynicism might be a clue to.

10. Elmer Hubbard: 'Men are not punished for their sins, but by them.' Which of your sins do you feel punished by? Are you still committing them? Why? Are the payoffs sufficient to offset the punishments? (Goethe said, 'A man does not mind being blamed for his faults, and being punished for them: but he becomes impatient if required to give them up.' Think about that, too, as you write.)

11. What would you do if you won the lottery? Would you really? Who would be the first person you'd want to tell? The last? In each case, why? Examine that awareness.

12. Dr Samuel Johnson: 'Where there is yet shame, there may in time be virtue.' Can you find the courage to write about a time in which you may have shamed yourself (*shame*, a big, lingering word, not *embarrassment*, a small, passing one). Can you now forgive yourself? Could you forgive someone else if they had done the same thing?

13. What is your favourite (non-sexual) fantasy? Could it ever come true? Do you do anything to make it come true? If not, why not? Really? What kind of person would you have to be to have that fantasy come true?

14. Begin your page with the words 'I wish ... ' and write, on that subject, every single thing that occurs to you – no matter how ludicrous, reprehensible or impossible it seems.

15. Can you remember the best gift you were ever given? What was so special about it? Who was it from? How old were you when you received it? Had you even known that you wanted it? Relish remembering the experience of getting just what your heart desired.

16. If you were suddenly to find yourself the subject of *This is Your Life*, what would you want them to say about you? What do you think they would say? Who would *you* choose to be the surprise guests to tell the world about you? What would you want them to tell? Who might expect to be called to talk about your life that you would *not* want? Why? How would you feel about being the subject of so much attention?

17. Simone Weil said, 'All sins are attempts to fill voids.' Think about this as you consider what voids you are trying to fill – and the sins you resort to in order to do so.

18. What do you consider the hardest thing you've ever had to accept in your life? Have you accepted it? Are you proud of the way you handled that time in your life? Would you deal with it differently now, if you could? In what way?

19. Write about what you consider to be the 10 greatest blessings of your life. This must be your *real truth*, not your idea of what you *ought* to feel. If you don't much care for your children but are delighted that you've kept your hair, tell yourself that.

20. 'It's no good running a pig farm for thirty years while saying, "I was meant to be a ballet dancer." By that time, pigs are your style.' Quentin Crisp. What kind of resonance

does that have for you? How would you define your style?
Does that please you? If not, how could you change it?
Will you?

21. Begin the page with the words 'I regret ...' and write on that subject as fully as you can.

22. Which of your vices cause you the greatest pain? Which give you the greatest pleasure? Do they tend to be the same? Which would you miss most if you gave up the vice – the pain or the pleasure?

23. Describe 'the perfect day' – all 24 hours of it.

24. May Sarton wrote, 'My faults too have been those of excess: I too have made emotional demands, without being aware of what I was asking. I too imagined that I was giving when I was battering at someone for attention.' Write about whatever vibrations and applications this may have for you.

25. Write about the first time you remember feeling proud of yourself. Was it something you said, did, thought? Write about what you are proudest of about yourself now. If you find this hard, examine whether it's because you don't allow yourself to feel proud, or because you don't feel you have much to be proud of. Does your pride depend on validation from someone else for you to be able to feel it?

26. Begin your page with the words, 'I am the sort of person who ...' and then write for 30 minutes on whatever comes into your mind on this topic. How do you feel about what you're saying?

27. Begin your page with the words, 'I am not the sort of person who ...' and then write for 30 minutes on whatever comes

into your mind on this topic. How do you feel about what you're saying?

28. Write about the angriest you can ever remember being. What triggered it? How did you handle it? Was it with someone else or with yourself? Are you still angry about it? If yes, what is that anger doing to or for you? If no, how did you resolve it? Is either behaviour a pattern you've used through your life?

29. 'The one thing I would change about myself would be ....' Oh, yeah? Then why don't you? What do you get out of holding on to that 'one thing'? Is it worth it? What would have to happen for you to feel that you could let go of it?

30. Jean Rostand said, 'We spend time envying people we wouldn't wish to be.' Think about who you envy and what it is that you envy about them. Would their life really make you happy? What is it that they have or are that you want to have or to be? *Could* you have or be those things? What do you have in their place? How do you really feel about that?

There. That's enough. The list of potential questions is endless, but the more you have to choose from, the more opportunity you'll have to dodge the ones that are most difficult for you to deal with – and you will already have realized that the hardest ones for you to write about are going to be the most valuable issues for you to examine. Never mind. The ones you skip now, you can always return to later when you're ready. For now you have 30 topics for 21 days. As you read through them each day, choosing what you will write on, just make a little tick to the side of the ones your mind shies away from. There will be information in those evasions which may be useful for you later.

In the meantime, remember your promise to yourself: you will write on one topic a day, each day, for three weeks. When you have finished each time, you'll put your writing away where no one else will see it, and *you will not look at it again either*. You're on your way.

CHAPTER 5

TAKING STOCK

It is easy to make a man confess the lies he tells to himself. It is far harder to make him confess the truth.

GEOFFREY HOUSEHOLD

O K. It is three weeks since you began your diary and, if all has gone well, you have collected at least 21 essays of self-discovery. Now is the time to consider what you have written.

I hope very much that you found the journal exercises intriguing, perhaps emotionally (not just mentally) absorbing, possibly even enlightening. Mostly, I hope you had the determination and the discipline actually to do them. With any luck, as you've gone about your life during these past weeks, you have continued to mull over what you found yourself writing, remembering things you thought you had forgotten, reevaluating what events meant to you when they happened, what they might mean to you now, considering some of the experiences of your life from a different perspective. If that has been happening, you're in a terrific position to begin this much more difficult phase of your self-discovery.

Because whether you found the writing itself a great treat or a great task, the telling of the story is always the easy part – no matter how much pain may be involved.

Now comes the hard part. This self-therapy you've embarked upon is going to demand of you two seemingly contradictory skills: the first is to experience your life fully – with all the passion and emotional investment that that implies – and the second, to be able to step aside from that same passion and involvement so that you can begin to see the patterns of your life. The goal of all the work that you have done, and that you will do, is to make clear to you what drives you. If you can't see it, you can't change it. Remember, too, that *change is a choice*. It may well be that as you become increasingly able to 'see your obvious' you'll decide you don't have any intention of giving up some of those aspects of yourself which are making your life uncomfortable. That is absolutely your decision to make. The purpose here is no longer to have your truths disguised from you.

As Søren Kierkegaard said, 'The majority of men are subjective toward themselves and objective toward all others, terribly objective sometimes, but the real task is, in fact, to be objective toward oneself and subjective toward all others.' Every page in this book is my attempt to help you in 'becoming objective toward yourself'.

Do not begin this until you can be sure of an extended period of uninterrupted privacy. When you *are* sure of that, grab something non-alcoholic to drink (you're aiming for some clarity here!), find a comfortable place to settle in and get out your work. You will also need something to write on and with. Whatever you're writing on, make two columns – one labelled 'Emotions', one 'Characteristics'.

A word as you begin. If you are a normal, neurotic person, you will probably have one of two responses to what you've written. Either you'll be depressed and a little disgusted by the person appearing on your pages or – and this is much more likely – you'll find yourself utterly enraptured by the fascinating individual whose life you're reading. For now, simply make a mental note of any rather generalized reaction and plough on. Whether it works better for you to jot down awareness as you go or to do it after you've read the entire body of your writing is unimportant. What is important is that you begin to acquaint yourself with yourself. That may sound absurd, but the fact is that most of us, even those who tend to be rather tiresomely introspective, carry around all sorts of assumptions, attitudes and beliefs about ourselves which may, in fact, bear very little relationship to the way we actually live our lives.

Begin, now, by considering the first of your categories: emotions. Under that heading, write a list of the feelings you are aware of experiencing as you read what you have written. The more specific you can be, the more exact your vocabulary, the more you will gain from this. For example, rather than describing yourself simply as 'happy', try to pin that down more precisely. Peaceful? Content? Satisfied? Elated? Joyous? Relieved? Comforted? Stimulated? Excited? Fortunate? Grateful? The list of possible words that might loosely fall under the rubric 'happy' is long, but each carries its own shade of meaning and your choice is vital information to you about you. If 'sad', again, be specific. Full of grief? Ashamed? Hurt? Pathetic? Moved? Nostalgic? Regretful? Humiliated? And so on. 'Sad' and 'happy' are, of course, only two of the most obvious responses. As you read, did you surprise yourself? Amuse yourself? Embarrass yourself? Did you feel angry, helpless, confused, hopeless, smug, remorseful, disgusted, self-pitying, compassionate, understanding, uneasy, impressed, loving? Those are only a few of the endless possibilities; many more should and will occur to you. Again, it is vital that you use all the emotional colours on your palette. Whatever you felt, whether or not that feeling makes sense to you, write it down.

When you have done that, turn to the column labelled 'Characteristics'. Again, use as fully, as specifically, and as honestly as you can the adjectives which describe to you the person you are meeting through your writing. Is that person easygoing? Unforgiving? Blaming? Self-blaming? Tolerant? Smug? Content? Responsible? Irresponsible? Witty? Judgemental? Frivolous? Serious? Self-protective? Cheerful? Angry? Withholding? Cold? Caring? Controlling? Controlled? Truthful? Easily offended? Compassionate? Gloomy? Stubborn? Accepting? You get the picture. If your list goes on for pages, if it is sometimes, even often, contradictory – all the better. You've given yourself just that much more information to deal with and to learn from.

By the time you have finished both the reading and the writing, you are probably more than ready to give all this a rest for a few days. At any rate, it is a good idea for you to do so. Because, although we will return to these essays of yours, approaching them in a slightly different way, for now it is necessary for your conscious and your subconscious mind to do some processing of what you've told yourself thus far. So take just a few moments to look over your two columns of words, as well as any other notes you may have made, then put your work away safely. Today's work is only the small, first step in your journey of self-discovery. But if you have approached it with interest, openness, emotional rigour and as much honesty as you can summon, you are truly well on your way. For the next few days write only if and as you want – on any topic which might engage you. There is no imperative to write at all, of course. However, my experience has been that if you break the habit you've established over the past three weeks, it will be that much more difficult to begin again when this week is up; when it will be time to move on to the next stage and the next chapter.

CHAPTER 6

MAKING PEACE WITH YOUR PARENTS

When I was a child, I spake as a child, I under-
stood as a child, I thought as a child: but when
I became a man, I put away childish things.

I CORINTHIANS 13:11

I t is time now to take a good look at your parents – your feel-ings about them and your relationship with them. Well, you *knew* it was coming. Whether you have felt blessed with your parents or cursed by them, you certainly don't need me to tell you that you cannot make peace with yourself until you have made peace with them, and peace with the lessons they taught you – lessons both about yourself and about the world in general.

In this relentlessly analytical age, anyone who is interested in a book of this kind may very likely already have invested years in picking over the 'problem' of their parents. By now you may be all too aware of the attitudes and values you absorbed from them as a child. In fact, you will have lived your life since either incorpo-rating most of those into your own reality or rebelliously acting in opposition to them. So doing a series of writings about those mes-sages is, I think, unlikely to plough any fertile ground, and might even reinforce some convictions of yours which would better benefit from a revised evaluation. That will come later. This week will be about forgiveness and transcendence, not blame.

Someone has said, 'To a child, the name for God is Father.' Leaving aside the issue of gender in that observation, I agree absolutely with it as a psychological truth. By the very nature of their role in your life, the shade cast by both your father *and* your mother is overwhelming. You can, of course, grow in that shade and find shelter there. But if you are to flourish, you will have to move out from under the shadow eventually, or your growth will be stunted. Until you can free yourself from the power of your parents – not the love, the *power* – you cannot be wholly yourself.

One of the many good reasons I know for having a child is that becoming a parent yourself allows you to forgive your own parents. (And if you do have children and haven't yet begun that process, you need to take a good, hard look at that.) Because parenting may be one of life's greatest blessings, but it is also unquestionably the hardest job anyone ever undertakes. If you are a parent, no matter how magnificently you succeed, you will also fail and fail again, every single day. Though 'to a child the name for God is Father', to the person doing the parenting that name is simply 'Human'. Often stressed, tired, unsure, irritable, frightened, impatient – these are just as much a part of the job description as the long list of positive attributes that also go with it, *Little Women* notwithstanding.

Whether or not you yourself have children, forgiveness and separation are the tasks at hand – tasks which you are absolutely capable of accomplishing. So here is the second truth that you must accept if you are to move on comfortably with your life: *there has to be a statute of limitations on blame.* This applies to every relationship in your life, whether the blame you've assigned has been to friends, lovers, siblings or to yourself. All of those associations will come up for review, but at this moment I ask you to consider that sentence only as it applies to your parents.

That there are some people who have suffered hideously at the hands of one or even both parents is inarguable and agonisingly tragic. But dealing with that degree of damage is beyond the scope of this book. What I do believe is that *most* parents are, at worst, as blinded, perhaps even as damaged, to exactly the same degree that we ourselves are. I also believe that they did the best they could with what they were at the time. That their 'best' may have been hurtful or wrong-headed or even harsh does not make that any the less true. If you are grown up enough to be reading this, you are also grown up enough to accept that your parents had, and have still, their own stories and their own reasons for their failures. And you are grown up enough (or are trying to be) to 'put away childish things', let go of the blame and move on. I hope these exercises will help you to do so.

Once again you will have one writing assignment each day for a week. Write for a minimum of 30 minutes each day, as before, but with these essays I implore you not to put your work away until you have said everything you need to say. Only when you feel a real sense of completion will it be time to stop. I stress this because, unlike the earlier exercises, these will be harder to evade by turning them into intellectual monographs. Unless you have had a cloudless, nearly conflict-free relationship with your parents, these may be rather difficult to write. I urge you to probe this subject as thoroughly and truthfully as you have it in you to do – and if it gets painful, don't give up! Write about the pain. I promise you, it will be worth it. So, tissues at the ready, get to work.

Day 1: Write a long letter to your mother. Whatever you feel the need to tell her, this is the place to do it. In this letter, express as truly and deeply as you can whatever you feel, or have felt but may not have been able to say before. Love, anger, frustration, pain, appreciation, pity, resentment, acceptance, understanding, jealousy, confusion, compassion, embarrassment – the possibilities are as vast and often as contradictory as human nature itself. For the purposes of this exercise, it does not matter whether your mother is living or dead – your feelings about her will still be very much alive. Remember, no one else but you need ever see this, so you are free to say *everything* you feel. If at some point you should decide to show the letter to your mother, that is a decision only you will be able to make (and then, only after much heart-searching), but do *not* write it with that aim in mind.

Remember, the purpose of all these exercises is to explore openly within yourself how you came to create the 'you' that you have become. If you use them only as excuses for venting spleen, even though that may help you to feel better for the moment, insight is unlikely and you might as well not have bothered to write them at all. The other option, of course, is that you will choose to write in a rosy glow of nostalgia, like the sundial which only counts the happy hours. This purely positive view will be no more useful than the other. Please, respect yourself enough to tell the entire truth as you perceived it.

Begin your letter with these words, 'As your child I feel ... .' And end it with these, 'Having said all that, if I could tell you only one thing, it would be ... .' Everything in between should come out of your most deeply felt awarenesses.

Day 2: Follow precisely the same guidelines, and write a letter to your father.

Day 3: For the first time I am going to ask you to move beyond your own personal perspective and perform an act of emotional imagination. Your assignment for today is to write a letter to yourself *as if* you were your own mother writing it – able to express all of her feelings to, and about, you. Begin with the words, 'As your mother I felt ... ', and end with, 'Having said all that, the one thing I want you to know is ... .'

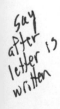

Follow exactly the same guidelines as you did in your two previous letters, but remain actively aware that your healing and development in writing this will come from the degree to which you are able to remove yourself, your feelings and your prejudices from what you write. Your aim here is to get inside your mother's mind so that you can understand what needs and dreams and demons drove her. The more you can move outside your own agenda and into your mother's, the richer your rewards. You do not have to agree with the way you think she would explain or define her point of view, but only when you begin to try to understand how *she* understands her reality can you forgive whatever there might be to forgive, and move from under her shadow with confidence in your own reality.

Say after letter is written

Day 4: Follow precisely the same guidelines as above, except this time the letter comes to you from your father.

Day 5: Write a second letter to your mother beginning with the words, 'I regret … ', and follow this with another, beginning, 'I appreciate … .' Now do the same two exercises as if your mother were writing to you.

Day 6: Write in the same manner as yesterday, but addressing the letters to and from your father.

Day 7: We began this chapter with a quote from the Bible, and it seems appropriate to end it with the same source – which tells us that the seventh day is a day of rest. However many days these letters actually took you to complete, if you did them with your deepest emotional commitment you may feel lighter, freer and more at peace than you have for many years. You may also feel emotionally exhausted. If these things are true for you, why don't you put this book away for a bit and give yourself a week or two simply devoted to living your life. Use that time, as well, to contemplate what you have learned from your writings so far and reflect on any new or deeper insights you may have gained through them. This is a time for what they call in the trade 'processing'.

If you don't want to break the habit of writing, this is a splendid opportunity to create some themes for yourself to play with on the page. Perhaps something you wrote earlier triggered an idea you want to examine more fully; perhaps you'd like to begin keeping a daily diary or to write a biographical sketch of one or both of your parents; maybe you'd like to write a thank you note to someone you've been remembering who influenced your life in a powerfully positive way. Whatever appeals to you, take a few weeks now to work to your own agenda. If you have children of your own, I urge you to do the same exercises you've just completed in regard to them. You know how to do it. As you write, and regardless of the age of the child involved, pay attention to the lessons you are teaching them through your actions, attitudes and example. Children learn what they live. Are your children learning what you want them to? Perhaps you'd like to do the same letter-writing to a sibling? Or a friend?

There are two proverbs which might be interesting for you to give some thought to during this time, considering whether either or both might have some application for your life. The first is Russian: 'The past is a long time ago, and anyway, it never happened.' How might recognizing the ways you may have distorted or misremembered your past help you to rid yourself of some of its baggage? The second is: 'It's never too late to have a happy childhood.' If you tend to think of your childhood as less than wonderful, how might you make that statement apply for you?

When you are ready to move on to the next step in your self-discovery, open this book again and begin the next chapter.

CHAPTER 7

MORE PEACE MAKING

If I am pressed to say why I loved him, I feel it can only be explained by replying: 'Because it was he; because it was me.'

MONTAIGNE

I hope very much that you are returning to this voyage of self-discovery with a real sense of excitement – and with the conviction that you are bringing to it some new awarenesses and deeper insights to aid you on your journey. This chapter will be the shortest one for me and probably the longest for you – but then, as I said at the start, all I can do is suggest possibilities and ask the questions. The answers are entirely up to you.

So. For however long it takes you to do this thoroughly, I ask you to follow exactly the same guidelines you used in the last chapter, this time directing your letters to and from your partner. (You might want to flip back to the last chapter to remind yourself about the details.) If you are not currently in a relationship, you can still gain from this exercise. Take this opportunity to re-evaluate a liaison in your past which had deep significance for you and see what you might be able to learn about it through writing about it now. With the perspective of time, you may discover new insights into a relationship which, even though it is over, may have left scars that have never completely healed.

If you have had other important relationships in your life which, even though they might have ended many years ago, still resonate powerfully for you, please find the time to do this same exercise in regard to them. The current physical presence of that person in your life is not at all necessary for their emotional impact to remain as potent as it ever was. This set of letters will be particularly valuable for you to do if you have been divorced, widowed or separated – regardless of whether your partnership was a legally recognized one or not.

1. Your first letter begins like this: 'As your partner [husband, wife, lover, whatever word is most comfortable for you] I feel ... .' Then – and *only* when you have expressed *everything* you feel necessary – end with, 'Having said all that, if I could tell you only one thing, it would be ... .'
2. The second letter comes from your partner to you, as you imagine they would write it if they could tell you *their* complete truth. Begin, 'As your partner I feel ... ', and end with, 'Having said all that, the one thing I want you to know is ... .'
3. Write a note to your partner beginning, 'I regret ... ', and another which begins, 'I appreciate ... .'
4. Write the same two notes, addressing them to yourself as you believe your partner would write if they were able to be completely honest with you.

The goal of these letters is similar to the objective you had when you wrote to your parents, but with this great difference: by their very nature, romantic relationships (especially ongoing ones) tend to be more fluid than those which exist between parents and their adult children. Because many of you will be in the middle of living the relationship as you are writing about it, you have a real chance to alter those areas you might find disturbing between you and your partner. For many adults, death has foreclosed that same opportunity with one or both parents.

So, whatever you have identified as needing attention, remember that unless you choose to do something about it, no amount of insight will make enough difference. Though it is true that if you can't see the problem you can't change it, sight alone is not enough. What are you going to do about it?

CHAPTER 8

SCRIPTING YOUR CHARACTER

*The important thing in acting is to be able to
laugh and cry. If I have to cry, I think of my sex
life. If I have to laugh, I think of my sex life.*
GLENDA JACKSON

I hope you won't be too disappointed to find that this chapter is not about sex but is, instead, about acting. More specifically, it is about the various tools actors use to bring a character to life on stage – some of which I think can be quite useful for you as you consider alternative ways to write the script of your own life. Besides, you've been doing some rather heavy-duty work so far, and I think it might be nice to have a change of tack for a bit.

In theory, we should all feel like the stars of our own lives. Certainly, at the very least, like its leading players. In practice, the neurotic is more likely to feel as if they have been cast against their will as a minor character in a play whose lines they haven't yet learned, working from a script they don't quite understand.

How about you? Do you feel well cast for the part you're playing every day? Who is directing you? Who wrote the script? You have, at the very least, collaborated on it. We'll look at that, too.

Actors begin their work with an analysis of the text. That's your cue to pull out your writing gear. In this chapter, you are going to start with an analysis of the text of your life, considering what you might be able to use from the actor's repertoire of skills to bring some new vitality and authenticity to the role you're playing.

The first question you must decide for yourself is what kind of play are you living? Comedy? Tragedy? Domestic comedy? Domestic tragedy? Farce? Melodrama? Bedroom farce? Kitchen sink drama? Mystery play? Problem play? Drawing room comedy? Comedy of manners? Theatre of the absurd? Social comment? Most of our lives contain elements of all of these at one point or another, but what you're looking for here is your perception of the *general tone* of your life. Pick a category, or devise one of your own, and consider that choice for a bit. Write a few lines to yourself about the classification you've chosen, your reasons for selecting it, and how you feel about that decision.

Now, ask yourself whether you've categorized your life in that manner because of the actual *events* of it, or because of your prevailing *attitude* toward it. You have just selected a label which you think defines the general tenor of your life. Does that label please you? Do you think the other people involved in your life would share that same view of it. Think hard and long before answering that question too easily. If you find that you must say truthfully that they would not, examine some of the reasons which might account for their difference of view. How would you feel about it if you decided that they might be right? What would be the advantages of learning to adopt a different perspective on the events of your life? The disadvantages? Take a few moments to write about this and we'll return to it later in the chapter.

Picasso said that art is a lie that makes us realize the truth. Every good play is not so much about plot as it is about the revelation or illumination of secrets, whether trivial or profound. The job of the playwright is to ask questions about life, and every actor's job is to attempt to find legitimate answers to those questions – particularly as far as his or her character is concerned. For the actor, rehearsals are a period of intense examination of the psychology of the role – as well as of those aspects of him or herself which will enrich, inform and vitalize that role.

Actors call this process 'building a character'. Whereas novelists generally give their readers direct insights into the minds and hearts of their fictional characters, playwrights do so only inferentially. Actors are not told what their characters think or feel – they must deduce it from three sources only: what that character says, what that character does, and what the other characters in the play say to and about that character (which may be highly suspect). From those clues only, it is the actor's job to create a fully realized human being on the stage.

Your own life surely deserves at least as much attention as an actor gives to the understanding of a part? And yet people rarely attend to their lives so closely, and certainly not so objectively. As part of your goal of 'seeing your obvious', I ask you here to approach your life as if it were a role you were undertaking for the first time. For this period at least, put aside the usual therapeutic technique of looking inward, and consider your persona and behaviours from the outside in – as a role you have chosen to play. Which is exactly the case.

Contemplate first this notion of 'building a character'. Although people often tend to see their personalities as something which just sort of evolved as a result of their genes and their givens – colour, class, gender, family, appearance, mental ability, etc., the fact is that you have been in the process of building your own character all of your life. And once you accept that as a fact and learn to view your creation clearly, you can alter it – and your interpretation of it – at will. For nearly 400 years there have been as many different Hamlets as there have been actors playing that part, but the script itself remains unchanged. In precisely the same way, if another person were asked to 'play' your life, *without altering any of its details*, its resonances and emphases would almost certainly be entirely different from those you bring to it. Who knows, another 'actor' might turn your tragedy into a comedy, or vice versa. More often than you may have considered, *interpretation* is everything.

This is the first lesson you can take from the theatre and then apply to your own life: almost every play can be presented as either a comedy or a tragedy, depending entirely upon the approach and emphasis the director chooses to give it. (Sometimes, of course, it is unintentionally funny or even tragic, but then, so is life.) What I want you to recognize is that the label you have put on your life is likely to be an arbitrary one. And since there is no objective right or wrong involved, doesn't it just make sense to choose to define your life in a way that pleases and satisfies you rather than the reverse? I've said this so often that you must be worn out reading it, but it cannot be stressed enough – you have it in your power to choose how you define the circumstances of your life. You may or may not always be able to alter those circumstances, but you can alter how you approach them. If your current attitudes aren't making you (or those you love) happy, do what actors do when their performances aren't working – look for a new interpretation and see what happens. (George Bernard Shaw, a man who knew a thing or two about theatre, said, 'Life does not cease to be funny when people die any more than it ceases to be serious when people laugh.')

Take a moment now to jot down half a dozen adjectives which you think would convey your 'character' to an actor playing you on stage. (You might want to refer back to the list you made in Chapter 5.) Unless you have some particular physical characteristic which must be considered, leave that aspect aside for now and simply concentrate on those descriptors which you think reflect your personality as you perceive it; i.e., light-hearted, stubborn, wilful, sullen, serene, gregarious, shy, etc. If you've really thought about this, some of your choices may seem contradictory – and that's as it should be. All of us are vastly complex and it is those complexities which give us interest.

When that's done, start a second list, recording all of those adjectives which you can remember other people having used about you through the years. Even if you completely disagree with them – particularly if you disagree with them – write them down. Some of these may be those off-the-cuff remarks friends and family have made from time to time which took you by surprise; some may have come out of an angry exchange (their having been said in anger does not necessarily invalidate them), and many will have been preceded by the words, 'Oh, you always . . . '! Really make an effort at remembering as you work on this column, keeping in mind that actors come to understand the truth of their characters through the observations of the other characters in the play, not just their own.

You will have already guessed that your next step is to compare the two lists and note the differences between your perceptions of yourself with the perceptions of others. The odds are that you will identify at least some gaps. If you have done the exercises in earlier chapters, you are already practised in the next bit; assessing, through your writing, just how you feel about this character whom you have built for yourself – that character as represented by your first list. Is it the person you intended to be? Does it please you? Depress you? Do you wish you could change the list? Expand it? In what way? What would be necessary for such a change to take place? Now look at your second list. Identify the disparities you've noted and consider carefully what truths they may hold. Do others see you more generously than you see yourself? Less so? Can you find some truth in the words which they have chosen to describe you? Can you at least understand why they might believe their descriptions to be true?

Combining the two lists, what character do you now see emerging from the page? Does the shoe fit? Does it pinch? Perhaps it's more comfortable, roomier, than your usual choice? Or tighter and less flattering? There is important information here if you've done your writing with honesty and clarity. Take a while to mull over what you have told yourself and make a note of any insights which seem important, or confusing, or disturbing.

The heart of most acting lies, not in the words the actors are given to speak, but in the truth they find between the lines – the sub-text. As the great actor Sir Ralph Richardson said, 'The most precious things in speech are the pauses.' This is one of the most useful lessons you can take from the theatre – an awareness of the sub-texts in your life. I know this is hardly a revolutionary con-cept. We all talk (often glibly) about hidden agendas. Usually we mean other people's, not our own. But it is this personal drive that an actor is trying to identify when talking about 'playing the in-tention'. Over and over every actor must examine and justify *why* his or her character says and does what the playwright has writ-ten – the purposes behind the words and actions. With each scene, with virtually each line in the play, the actor must deter-mine just what his or her character is attempting to accomplish. And the more specific each such decision is, the richer the per-formance will be. For example, if the scene takes place at a cocktail party, it is not enough for the actor to say that the goal of the character is 'to have a good time'. Is the character's true goal to establish a place in society? To begin a love affair? To learn more about some other person at the party? To fill time in an empty life? To provide distraction from a worrying problem? To establish superiority over the rest of the crowd? The possibilities are limited only by the needs of the script, but each answer to each 'why?' will add another layer to the actor's understanding of the role. As the actor comes to realize his or her part more com-pletely, many of the earlier, more obvious answers to that 'why?' will deepen in resonance or alter altogether, giving new richness and complexity to the part being built.

This same kind of assessment is essential for us if we are to see the obvious in our own lives. Please note: I am asking you here to consider your *intentions*, not your emotional responses. Psychology has provided us with more than enough theories to employ in our tireless – and often tiresome – efforts to consider the reasons behind our responses. It has done less well in focusing on those choices we make which reflect our, perhaps unacknowledged, intentions. One of the truest and most astonishing insights in the field of psychology was made by Thomas Szasz when he wrote, 'To the mental patient's family, his illness is a problem. To the patient himself, it is a solution.' Actors must continually ask themselves, 'What "problem" are these characters trying to solve for themselves through their behaviour?' You could not have a more powerful insight to use in your own attempt at self-understanding. As you go through your days, I encourage you to challenge yourself often with this question, 'What problem am I trying to solve for myself in doing this? Is it working? Might there be a better way to achieve the same goal?'

I've already stated my conviction that most of our problems and hang-ups result from simple bad psychological habits – lazy or misguided or outmoded patterns of belief and assumption which we developed long ago and have simply never reassessed or attempted to change. It's no wonder that we can't see our obvious, we so rarely look for it! Most of us drift from one experience to another, either led by someone else's agenda for us or by our own long-established emotional habits, without ever questioning very seriously what we hope to achieve for ourselves through our actions. At other times, we may even be aware of a compulsion to behave in a certain way, but shy away from investigating the underlying need which is driving that compulsion. To admit clearly to ourselves that we *do* want, exactly *what* we want, and how *badly* we want makes us feel terribly vulnerable. Nevertheless, I urge you to take this from the actor's bag of tricks: work on becoming aware of your intentions as specifically as if you were interpreting a role.

For a week, do this for your writing exercise: at the end of each day, jot down what you have done that day, considering each activity from the standpoint of your underlying purpose for doing it. When you have identified that goal, ask yourself how well the given activity helped you in, or perhaps hindered you from, reaching your goal. Remember, 'God is in the details'. If you've worked for money, or if you've cooked a meal for your family, it is not enough to say 'My intention was to put food on the table.' You owe yourself a much more thorough exploration than that, and by now you certainly know how to do it. Just remember to keep peeling back the layers. If your initial instinct is to say 'I did such and such, which I didn't want to do, because if I didn't __ would be mad at me', respect yourself enough to go beyond the simplistic conclusion that your intention was 'not to have a fight', and dig to discover whatever deeper, wider truths may be implicit in that need to avoid such confrontation. Like the actor who uses each rehearsal to understand his or her character more fully, use these writings to discover your true agenda for your life – *your* agenda, not anyone else's. This will demand some ruthless honesty on your part, requiring you to *own* your personal needs and ambitions, not evading those truths by shifting the impetus for your actions onto someone else. Jean-Paul Sartre said, 'Do you want to know who you are? Act. Action will delineate and define you.'

Still working from the outside in on this role you've created for yourself, professional actors learn quickly to be very dispassionate about the 'self' they project, accepting that the type they represent will have both its assets and its limitations. Think for a moment – as objectively as possible – about your 'type' as a casting director would perceive it. If someone were to play you on stage or film, who do you think they would cast to do so? (Be realistic here!) Write down a few of the qualities you think you share with that actor or actress which might account for such a choice, recognizing that 'type' has less to do with actual physical resemblance than it does with style, attitude and presentation. (Goldie Hawn and Meryl Streep are both good-looking blondes of much the same age, but their 'types' are clearly very different. Jack Nicholson and Mel Gibson are both popular leading men, their 'types' very dissimilar.) Now, staying within your age range, write down the name of the performer you *wish* would be chosen to portray you. As you do so, consider whether your choice would be the same one you think the casting director would make. If not, write down those characteristics which you think would *preclude* your favourite from being selected to play you. As you work on this, try to put fantasy aside as much as possible, and don't get bogged down by choosing some performer whose good looks are in a class all their own – unless yours are as well. Remember, you are going to be as clear-eyed about your looks as actors must struggle to be about theirs. What I'm hoping you will identify here is how closely you are in touch with the 'you' the world sees.

By now you have established your type. Is there a disparity between the persona you present and the one you would like to present? If so, have you identified it? Every actor knows how to alter the impression they give by adopting different hairstyles, clothing and make-up. Take a few moments to give yourself a long, candid look in the mirror. Then do a thorough mental inventory of your wardrobe. It makes absolutely no difference whether you've had millions or only pennies to spend, every item you own is a reflection of your perception of yourself – or of the desire you have for yourself. Does the personality you see in the mirror, do the clothes hanging in your wardrobe, reflect the person you want to be? If not, why did you choose them? Does your wardrobe contain items which you never wear because you don't have the nerve? In what way? How would you have to change to dare to wear them? When did you decide that you were the person reflected by the clothes you wear most often? Did someone else make that decision for you? Would you like to change that reflection? Could you? Why don't you? Write down your observations and responses to this.

It is an interesting quirk of human nature that people often assume that simply because someone is famous, we should be flattered to be told we are like them. It's been my experience that the reverse is usually the case – regardless of how good-looking and well-loved that celebrity might be. If you can remember similar uncomfortable comparisons made about you, make a note of them and consider what it was that displeased you. What is it about that celebrity you do not like? What quality or qualities do you wish you did not share with them? (Remember, physical resemblance may be the least important factor in that analogy.) Even if you were insulted or depressed by the comparison, can you be objective enough to understand why it might have been made? What could you alter about the way you present yourself so that such a similarity would not be noted again?

Jean Rostand said, 'We alone know that those whom we really resemble are not at all those whom we seem to resemble.' When you have finished working on this chapter, I encourage you to incorporate the notes you've just made into a more complete examination of the gap between what you perceive yourself to be and the way you present that self to the public. Could you close that gap? How and why do you prevent its closing? Is it possible that your 'type' is simply the result of habits of attitude and perception about yourself which are no longer valid? (Think for a minute of Ginger Rogers in her last years – well into her 80s and still wearing the hair, make-up and fashions of her 30-year-old self.) Remember too, that although most actors have learned to assess their types pretty realistically, they have also learned to explore the enormous range of possibilities contained within that classification. You needn't be any more limited than they are.

If, as you work on this, you decide that, actually, your type suits you just fine, congratulate yourself and then try to think of ways you might at least expand its dimensions. If, however, as you work on this, you decide yours does not suit you well at all, write down a list of those alterations you might make which would bring the self you present and the self you'd like to be closer together. You are no different than a good actor – in Walt Whitman's words, 'I am large – I contain multitudes.' Acknowledge that same truth for yourself. How about liberating some of those aspects of yourself that you've kept hidden – perhaps so hidden that you weren't even aware that they were in there? The way you'll feel about yourself if you do so might amaze you. What will also amaze you is how differently other people will respond to you when you present them with your altered self. Many actors say they never really understand the character they are playing until they've finally got into the costume and make-up of the part. What new 'costume' appeals to you? How about trying it on for a while to see what happens? And then, perhaps, trying a few more? Once you've formed a clear vision of the character you're becoming (or refining, or creating) you'll be immensely helped in your goal if you remember always to dress the part.

What follows now are some further actors' techniques to help bring your character to life as you live it daily. Why not try incorporating one or two into your life and see if by doing so you can add some dimension and texture to that character which is yourself? Write about the results of these experiments, considering what surprises you may have discovered as a consequence. How did your friends and family respond? Do you enjoy this enlarged sense of yourself? Will you keep it up?

1. A recurring theme of this book is to learn to live 'as if', until you are able to make that 'as if' your reality. When you can't find your courage and courage is called for, when confidence

is vital and only insecurity is available, when you've been hurt and it is the worst possible moment for crying out, that's the time to steal from the actor's repertoire and behave as *if* you were brave or confident or carefree. If you can act it, for that moment at least, you can be it. And who knows, in time, you might just become it.

2. The better the actor, the more humour they will bring to a part – and that applies even when they're playing characters as overwhelmingly tragic as Oedipus or Medea. If they can find flashes of humour in even the darkest of roles (and the good actors can), surely you can remember to look for the comic moments during your own dark times. Like everything else in life, humour is often an act of will, and recognizing it just another habit of thought. Remember, too, what George Bernard Shaw said about changing tragedy into comedy simply by having the characters sit down. When your drama is escalating out of all proportion, why not grab a chair and try to find the comedy? And since, as someone else has said, comedy is simply tragedy plus time, doesn't it make sense to telescope the miserable times as small as possible and move as quickly as you're able to the humour of the situation?

3. Sometimes life becomes, in Hamlet's words, 'weary, stale, flat and unprofitable'. There may be no obvious cause, but the zest has gone out of things for you. When those times come, consider how every actor must feel when he or she has said the identical words and performed the identical actions every day for months on end. For actors, keeping their jobs depends on keeping at least the appearance of energy and

newness night after night after night. However sick they may be of the part they're playing, actors do not have the luxury of allowing that to show. To keep their sanity, they must develop techniques to make the stale fresh again. The actor's constant challenge is to bring a new vision to an old view by looking for previously unconsidered aspects of their character, experimenting with different pace and emphasis, searching for humour in unexpected places, altering their reactions to the other characters, responding in new ways to old stimuli – and then remaining open to the surprises which inevitably follow these subtle shifts. In acting as in life, habits of response build up which must be challenged over and over again if vitality and engagement are to remain possible.

4. Actors talk about 'staying in the moment' – the struggle never to anticipate and to allow themselves to be surprised. Since, obviously, they know not only what their character is going to say next, but what all the other characters are going to say as well, their problem becomes how to approach each scene, each word in each scene, as if it had never happened before. Actors will attest that, when they do succeed in accomplishing this internally (and not just for the benefit of the audience), some kind of alchemy – some unexpectedness, some unexplored insight or deeper understanding – takes place. By 'staying in the moment', by not anticipating what they know is to follow, by truly listening (and listening *freshly*) to the other actors' lines, something new is allowed to occur.

We face the same challenge in our own lives. Whether in personal or professional relationships, the human tendency is to waste enormous emotional energy anticipating what we assume is going to come next. Like the actor who knows the play by heart, we sabotage ourselves and our relationships by being sure that we already know what the other person is going to say before they even have a chance to say it. Instead of actually listening to them, we spend the time they are talking planning what we're going to say in response to words which haven't even been voiced yet. And yet, even if their words do turn out to be precisely the ones we expected, by anticipating them and therefore not really hearing them as they are said, we have closed ourselves off from any possibility of finding fresh surprises within and behind the words themselves.

Many of the most destructive patterns of human interaction are the result of just this kind of unhearing response to each other. It is no wonder our arguments tend to be so repetitive and circular – we are each deafened to the other by the noise of our expectations. The next time you find yourself at the start of an old, old situation with someone, you might approach it as if you were an actor struggling to stay in the moment, without anticipating or prejudging the outcome. This is the time to repeat to yourself the phrase which every new actor learns like a mantra: 'Acting is reacting' – and that means reacting *anew* to what is actually occurring, not to what you have already decided is going to occur. Even a minor shift of perception may effect a major change in your response to some very tired dialogue.

5. Find your light. One of the first things every actor learns when stepping onto a stage at the start of their career is to find where their light is, and then to make sure they stay in it. If the audience can't see them, all their work is for nothing. If you've ducked out of your own light for too long, or if you have allowed the people and/or circumstances of your life to keep you too much in the shadows, set about considering the degree of attention that fits your comfort level and then begin to look for ways of achieving that attention. If, on the other hand, you're beginning to suspect from your writings that you are rather guilty of some scene stealing yourself, it might well behove you to begin to move over enough for other people to share the spotlight. Even the greatest actors have a hard time sustaining a one-person show for long!

6. Actors adore playing heroes; villains are enormously satisfying (naturally, since they offer a wonderful opportunity to loose one's Shadow safely); and almost always playing the fool is great fun. But the actor who deserves your sympathy is the one assigned the thankless task of playing the insecure, self-pitying whiner. The best they can hope for is to make it a comic turn – and the script does not always allow for this. Nothing is duller or more irritating to an audience than the character who is a pathetic sniveller. If this behaviour is a pattern you've adopted for yourself (though no doubt you've labelled it a little less harshly), face that truth honestly and then give some cold, hard thought to just how fascinating *you* find such characters when you meet them in fiction or in real

life. Not a pretty picture, is it? Then why not begin deciding how you might get your needs met through more positive and appealing methods? Remember, it's love you're hoping for, not pity. Anyway, whiners are damned lucky if they do get pity – their ploys are much more likely to be met with contempt. Remember, 'habit is overcome by habit' and if this is one of the neurotic habits you've fallen into, your job is to act as if you had confidence and self-sufficiency, until it is finally extinguished. Then, as you won't need your pity yourself, you can give it to the poor actor instead!

7. Perhaps the one factor which separates the really fine actors from their more average colleagues has to do with the mastery of timing. The great ones know how to hold a pause so that it can seem to carry the full weight of a conversation, how to reflect rather than just rushing into a reaction, how to control the audience's laughter so that important words aren't lost, how to vary their pace and energy to keep the crowd's interest alive. We face precisely the same problem in living our lives. How often have you hurried into a confrontation with someone important to you because you were too impatient to wait for a better time or setting? Or chattered nervously – and foolishly – rather than taking a moment to gather your scattered wits? Or let impulsive words fly instead of taking a breath and considering what you really want to say, and how you want to say it? Or given into the comforts of habit and inertia rather than making the effort to bring some zest and enthusiasm into your dealings? Or perhaps you've lost your nerve and let the perfect moment go when it presented itself?

An actor's sense of timing comes from an intense awareness of their audience – and if we paid as much attention to our audiences as good actors do to theirs, we might achieve their same success. But most of us are much too busy trying to further our own agendas to be as sensitive as we should be to the other people involved with us. The result usually is that we not only lose our audience, we lose the points we are trying to make with them, too. For the next week or so, why don't you try experimenting with your timing, as if the effectiveness of your 'performance' depended on it. Who knows? It just might.

8. We have all heard stories of the nerves almost all actors suffer from just before they step on stage. Many of them will even admit to a consuming terror which causes them to vomit or to tremble so violently that they can scarcely apply their make-up. Why are they willing to go through such tortures, in some cases for every night of the run of the show? Because they have learned the truth of Fritz Perls' observation that the real basis for fear is excitement. Perls recommends that when you are afraid, take a deep breath and allow yourself to *taste* the excitement hiding behind your anxiety. Actors have learned that when the play finally begins and they are at last on stage, that stage-fright will be submerged in the exhilaration of their performance. This fear question is covered more thoroughly in a later chapter, but until you get to it, how about trying Perls' technique for yourself, the next time you are dreading something you can't avoid facing?

9. Love your character. Above everything else, this is the actor's first task – and your first and over-riding task as well, as you

consider the character you've built for yourself up till now. If an actor cannot love the part he or she is asked to play – not necessarily approve of, but love – they will never succeed in bringing that role to life. Full stop. And this is where you have the advantage over actors as you go about living your life, because an actor must deal with the part he or she is given. They must find some humanness to love even in those characters whose behaviours are reprehensible, whose morals are indefensible and whose only chance of redemption is dependent on the will of the playwright. They do this by coming to as deep an understanding of the role as the text and their own insights will allow, by discovering for themselves what problems their characters think they are solving by those behaviours, and through acknowledging that no human emotion is foreign to any of us.

Your own life script is a work-in-progress. You have it in your power to rewrite your conduct, your attitudes, even your persona as you decide necessary. So give yourself a break. Every exercise in this book is an exercise in understanding. You may or may not find yourself lovable in some of the ways you would choose to be at the moment. But the more deeply you come to understand yourself, the more you will be able to forgive yourself and make that love possible. If you can't quite feel sure that you deserve it yet, it is time, once again, to live 'as if' until you can make it true.

CHAPTER 9

TAKING NOTE

If you jot down every silly thought that pops into your head, you will soon find out everything you most seriously believe.

MIGNON McLAUGHLIN

Most of us carry around the most astonishing notions about ourselves; at least they certainly seem to astonish the people who know us best if we happen to claim certain qualities as our own. Perhaps it is our fancy that we are deeply philosophical, even intellectual – and yet our friends would describe (and perhaps even love us for) our scattiness. Or vice versa. Maybe we pride ourselves on our compassionate understanding, though other people have been heard to mutter 'intolerant' under their breaths when speaking about us. And so on. As neurosis is the inability to see the obvious, it's hardly surprising that this should be so.

In your ongoing quest to make this obvious available to you, try this for the next week: keep a note pad near you and concentrate, without being compulsive about it, on doing just what Ms McLaughlin suggests in the quote above. Simply make a note of as many of your random considerations and responses as possible. Not an essay, just a quick observation. Don't bother noting thoughts about the minutiae of life – picking up clothes from the cleaners, adding milk to the shopping list, making a dentist's appointment, etc. (However, if you find that the preponderance of your thoughts are these kinds of necessary unimportances, that awareness should be a flashing alarm to you to try to discover just what you're avoiding by focussing on such trifles.) Work on becoming mindful of those knee-jerk responses, judgements, dreams, fantasies, memories and idle speculations which drift in and out of your mind, and which define you. Be as vigilant as possible.

For instance, if you begin to notice that every time you see someone on the street, you immediately do a quick mental assessment of them, note that fact – the fact of the *assessment*, not the assessment itself. Is your every encounter an unconscious competition, weighing mentally which of you is winning? If so, are the conclusions you reach likely to leave you feeling superior? Inferior? What do you get out of an approach to life which is always either one up or one down? If you were to find no one to compare yourself to, favourably or otherwise, what or who would you be left with? Are you truly no more than a plus or minus in relation to somebody else?

Do you find yourself mentally replaying some rather unimportant slight or grievance which might better have been discarded long since? What are you getting out of holding on to it?

Perhaps you begin to realize that your commitment to your work is so all-consuming that human contact barely registers with you at all? Do you operate from an invariable impatience with what you perceive to be the incompetence of the rest of the world? Do you tend to find yourself amused by life? Irritated? Impatient? Moved? Driven? Depressed? Peevish?

What are you discovering to be your general expectations? Do you assume that the world will be chiefly kind? Hostile? Indifferent? Are you more superstitious than you realized? More trusting? More suspicious? Cynical? Fretful? Do you worry more than you realized? Less than you thought? Do you tend to anticipate friendliness or at least civility in your daily dealings? The reverse? Do you exist in a cloud of fantasy? A swarm of trivia? Do you find yourself living in a memory of the past? A dream of the future? The possibilities for discovery and surprise are limitless if you really follow through with this – and the rewards of insight are immense.

At the end of your week, gather up all your scattered observations, examine what you have written and try to discern what picture you see emerging. Then, as if you were trying to describe a character in a novel, write in the third person a sketch of that person who appears in your notes. What does that character seem to believe? What seem to be the assumptions on which they act?

Can you recognize that person in yourself? How do they match the person you have described as yourself in all of your previous writings? Are they someone you would like to know? *Are they someone you are glad to be?*

If the answers to any of those questions is 'no', give serious thought to that awareness, and then put your work (and this book) aside for a day or two – time enough, at least, to let your subconscious get to work on this realization. Then, when you're ready, take out this exercise again and evaluate what you see there. Then write a thorough analysis of just what you plan to do about the disparities you've noted.

It is becoming an old familiar song by now, but you have it within your power to alter whatever aspects of your character are making your life displeasing. Remember, we are addressing your character here. There may not be much you can do about your genetic givens, or even your circumstances, but your character is *your* unique creation. If it matters enough to you, you can recreate it. It won't be easy and it won't be fast, so concentrate first on those characteristics which you most desire for yourself, and experiment with *behaving* as if they are an authentic part of you: in time they will become so.

CHAPTER 10

THE SHADOW

If you hate a person, you hate something in him that is part of yourself. What isn't part of our-selves doesn't disturb us.

HERMAN HESSE

R ead that quote through several times, paying attention as you do to whatever feelings it might arouse in you. For a little while, simply allow your mind to drift over those people in your life whom you find the most maddening or upset-ting, jotting down their names as they occur to you. These will not be your pleasantest few minutes, no doubt, but they could end up being very valuable to you.

In essence Hesse's statement mirrors, though in much more ac-cessible terms, Carl Jung's concept of the Shadow, which Jung believed to exist in all of us. In Jung's construct, the Shadow refers to the whole of those particular characteristics which we our-selves possess, but which we hide from the world and, even more dangerously, have hidden from ourselves. Again, 'What isn't part of ourselves doesn't disturb us.'

The work of this chapter is to try to get in touch with

your Shadow, own it, and see how its projection has influenced (and perhaps poisoned) various relationships in your life. This is much harder than it sounds – not simply because we all expend enormous mental energy in trying to bury our dark sides – but because we are apt to scratch like cats rather than accept that those same qualities which we despise in other people are alive within ourselves.

This concept of the Shadow is a tough one to deal with, not because it's difficult to grasp, but because it can manifest itself in so many different ways, depending on our particular personal hang-ups.

Here is just one possible example of the Shadow's effects: many people find themselves both drawn to and then repelled by those very characteristics which they find most despicable in themselves. So we might have one member of a couple who is in such need of the world's approval that she is unable to express her anger or need for control, always presenting herself as thoroughly 'nice' – charming, compliant, agreeable, non-threatening. (This particular manifestation of the anger issue is much more common in women than in men, though hardly exclusive to them.) When she then chooses a partner who expresses both anger and a determination to control vehemently and often, she has, in fact, at some level chosen that very person *because* of their willingness to express those things – a sort of vicarious outlet for her emotions. She is only conscious of feeling mortified and appalled by the 'reprehensible' behaviour of her partner. Since she, as the 'good' half of the couple, has hidden her Shadow's agenda from herself completely, she lives in a constant state of turmoil and unhappiness at what she perceives to be her partner's faults. This is a typical pattern, and if it happens to be one of yours, even though your specifics may be altogether different, the pattern itself will be the same.

Can you identify any parallels for this dynamic in one or more of your own relationships? Think about this closely, but do not limit your consideration only to your partner. Do you have a child whose personality causes you special difficulty? Could it be your Shadow which you sense thriving in that child? Or perhaps it's a friend whose behaviour both fascinates and disturbs you? A parent? An employer? A colleague? If you can distinguish such a component in one or more of these associations, write about it, searching for some illumination of those disguised aspects of your own character which those alliances might reveal. Be careful not to fall into an analysis only of what you perceive to be the other person's 'faults', or the problems which exist between the two of you as a result. This exercise is *not* about the other person or your relationship with them. It is about *you*. What you're digging for here is a clear recognition of those traits in that other person which most disturb you, and the ways in which those traits might be a reflection of your own hidden dark side. What do those people allow themselves to feel and to express that you both desire and disallow for yourself? Perhaps it is not the specific feelings themselves that you are hiding, but the belief that you have any right to express any 'unacceptable' feelings at all?

As you work on this, it's essential that you remember that one person's despicable might be another person's desirable. Characteristics which leave you wincing with disapproval, someone else with a different set of aversions may not even notice, and may, in fact, enjoy and/or respect. *Because those characteristics which may appal you are not necessarily bad in themselves. They are simply incompatible with the way you have decided that you want to be in the world and with the value system you hold.* Be unrelenting with yourself as you work on this. Concentrate on those traits you dislike most intensely in others, and then listen very carefully for their echoes in yourself before you discount the possibility that those same qualities may also reside in you.

Remind yourself that many of the things you are averse to may simply result from your specific cultural background and inculcation. Attitudes and behaviours which are acceptable or even desirable in one country may be considered quite appalling in another. What one culture represses, another expresses lustily. And that doesn't just apply to matters sexual. Does that make your society right and theirs wrong? S.I. Hayakawa wrote, 'If you can see in any given situation only what everyone else can see, you can be said to be so much a representative of your culture as to be a victim of it.' Consider this, too, as you write.

A note before I continue: if you work on this seriously, it will very likely be one of the most challenging and disturbing matters that you will deal with in your task of self-discovery. Facing your Shadow demands that you acknowledge your most deeply covert, shameful or embarrassing characteristics. But that may not be the hardest aspect of this for you: by recognizing those qualities in yourself, you will be forced by your own common sense to let go of some of the harsh judgements you may have made about other people who exhibit those traits openly – and with that, your own sense of moral superiority. (In the next chapter we'll look more closely at this question of the general need most of us have to feel superior, because of our underlying fear that we are actually inferior.) You are not required, of course, to learn to see those shared characteristics as admirable, but you must at least accept that they are not altogether foreign to you. Talk about a blow to the ego!

Many years ago I was told that I was guaranteed true emotional and spiritual growth if I had the courage to pray for an ego-shattering experience. The idea absolutely terrified me and I certainly never considered trying any such thing. Since then, however, time and life have taught me that you get such experiences whether or not you have the courage to pray for them. That being true, don't, for *your* sake, dismiss this chapter with the fatuous, facile argument that 'That whole Shadow thing is absurd! I don't have to be a secret Hitler to abhor what he did! I don't have to be a secret child abuser to know that abuse – any abuse – is hateful and wrong! I don't have to be a thief to know that stealing is wrong!' Since you are not stupid, you are certainly capable of appreciating the difference between moral outrage and a personal aversion. This is not about abstract principles. It is about extremely personal antagonisms.

Here is another way for bringing a different aspect of your Shadow to the surface for examination. We all find ourselves in various groups throughout our lives – social, professional, familial, civic, whatever. Think of the men and women who comprise these groups and try to identify one or two whom you simply cannot bear. Concentrate on someone whose personality or style of presentation you find intensely irritating, perhaps for reasons you don't quite understand – or possibly for reasons which you think you already understand all too well!

Write a brief summary of those characteristics which make that person especially odious to you. Now examine those traits with the same challenge to yourself which you set above. Remind yourself, in the psychologist's phrase, to keep 'peeling the onion'. For instance, when doing this kind of analysis people often write something like this: 'She is such an appalling show-off. The way she dresses! She dresses like a tramp! Everything she does is just a scream for attention. She's always fighting for the spotlight! I certainly do *not* want to dress that way! In fact, I wouldn't be caught dead with her hair, her clothes or her make-up. And that's not my damned "Shadow" talking. It's just a simple statement of truth.' That is a typical response to this exercise – heading right into the forest and tripping over the tree roots! Since, however, the above is not likely to be your particular concern, but is merely a hypothetical situation, you will have noticed immediately what that person did not – that the issue involved in that scenario is unlikely to have anything at all to do with this person's secret desire to dress like the woman described. What it may have to do with, though, is a hidden longing for attention – or perhaps even the longing to feel entitled to *demand* it. It might have something to do with an unrecognized desire to express a more flamboyant aspect of her personality than the relentlessly 'ladylike' one she has always adopted.

To borrow another hypothetical example: 'He thinks he knows everything. He's always trying to tell us how we could do things better and he wants to run everything. In fact, he's not one bit cleverer than the rest of us, so who does he think he is, thinking

his ideas are so much better than ours?! Who elected him God?'
Play with that example mentally for a bit and, since it is not one
you're involved in yourself (maybe), see what sense you might
make of it if that person asked for your insights.

Perhaps this is a good time to reiterate what I said at the beginning of this book. No matter how much training a therapist
has, they don't 'know' anything more about yourself than you do
and, in fact, it's almost certain that they know a great deal less.
I can't tell you what your 'truth' is, any more than I (or anyone
else) can tell you what your behaviours and feelings 'mean'. The
only things psychological training and experience can offer are a
basis for some educated guesses for ways to consider possibilities,
and a caution to the therapist to stay out of the client's way while
the *client* does the work. I say all that only to remind you that in
this work on the Shadow (or on any other issue), there are no
right or wrong answers. All of these exercises are only avenues
which, I hope, will lead you down your own personal road towards seeing your obvious. You alone have the ability to uncover
your Shadow. But once you have faced your dark side and the ego
jolt that comes with it, you will have gained some powerful
knowledge about yourself, which you can use to liberate some important aspects of your personality that you have denied yourself
– perhaps all of your adult life.

This is another instance of my belief that many of those things
which cause us the greatest psychological difficulty are often only
the consequence of habits of attitude and conviction which no
longer have any real relevance for us. Perhaps they never did. So
much of what we believe and assume has come to us secondhand.

All through our lives our parents, friends, teachers, lovers – anyone who has influenced us deeply – have passed on to us their own values, and we have too often accepted them, internalized them, and then lived as if they were our own, without ever challenging their validity for our own lives. And we have had the same impact on other people in their lives, too, presumably. The point is, we have all accepted as 'fact' a number of vicarious opinions about what is acceptable behaviour – what is 'good' or 'bad' – without ever considering or, with adulthood, reconsidering whether those positions actually make sense for us. This accounts for many of those 'Shadow' aspects we fear in ourselves.

Let's go back for a minute to the example above of that woman who could not, or would not, express her anger because people might not like her if she did. Now, it hardly takes a psychologist to know that anger is a completely normal, human emotion, and often the only rational response to a given situation. But if this woman was taught at a young age that her anger was not only unacceptable but morally wrong as well, it is absolutely predictable that she would have learned early on to swallow such feelings and her reactions to them. In time she might even truly believe that she no longer felt that anger. But such lessons are very indigestible and, however hard we swallow, they remain inside us and continue to lurk in our unconscious, causing all sorts of mental havoc. That particular woman was frightened and ashamed of her entirely healthy anger. What might *you* have decided was 'wrong' with you? Could you be wrong about that 'wrong'? Since you are reading this as a normal, neurotic human being it is extremely unlikely that your Shadow conceals a repressed axe murderer. So what are you afraid of discovering about yourself that's so dreadful? And who decided it was dreadful anyway – you or somebody else? Even if, upon mature reflection, you continue to feel uncomfortable about some quality you bring to light, you'll have reason for self-congratulation that you have learned to control your open expression of it. You might even be able to find some compassion and understanding (instead of blame) for other people who share that quality without your restraint.

Anyone interested enough in the subject of psychology to be reading this book will probably already be familiar with what psychologists mean when they talk about 'projection' – that unconscious (and often inaccurate) transfer of our own attitudes, feelings and responses onto another person. Though each act of projection is not *necessarily* a function of the Shadow, it very often is. Look at those names on your list again and consider them from a slightly different angle; this time in terms of the ways in which you might be projecting your own unacknowledged dark side onto them. Could it be, in fact, that the competitiveness in that person that drives you crazy is, in reality, your own? The bossiness? The controlling? Attention seeking? Selfishness? Self-pity? Insensitivity? For your purposes you need only focus on those qualities you've already enumerated as anathema to you personally. No matter how obnoxious other people may find different aspects of those people you've named, your only concern here is with those specific traits which actually disturb *you*. Your job now is to assess – in writing – whether it is possible that what you are responding to in those people is, in truth, your own reflection in their mirror. You may discover that they actually have less of that disturbing trait than you had assumed. They may even have more. Either insight is immaterial. Once again, you are not looking at them through this work, but at yourself.

See what I mean about the complex possibilities inherent in this subject? From experience with my clients (and myself) I can attest to the benefits of doing and evaluating the work of these exercises. But I hope it is also implicit that your journey of self-discovery will continue long after you've put aside both book and pen. As you go about your life, the next time you find yourself responding to someone with intense irritation, take a breath, grab your writing materials, and consider what that irritation might be a clue to in your own subconscious.

Now for the good news. If consciousness of the thorny side of your Shadow is making you uneasy, you need also to know that there is a more positive aspect to that same Shadow within you – the side that has to do with your unrealized, untapped potential. Several times I have encouraged you to live 'as if', until some quality you admire (but have not exhibited much in the past) becomes your own. You may have felt that that was a pretty simplistic suggestion and much easier said than done. I agree only with the second part of that sentence. I have never suggested that change is easy. You didn't become what you are in an instant and you won't alter that quickly either. But you certainly can do it. Pay close attention to those qualities you most admire in others, but believe you lack yourself.

The very fact of your admiration is a sure clue that those qualities also reside in you, even if at this time they are hidden in your Shadow. *Living 'as if' is not a matter of pretending to be something you are not, but of practising exhibiting those characteristics which you have not allowed expression in the past.*

Each technique in this book has been designed to encourage you in different ways of perceiving and reflecting upon the experiences of your life. Whether it is a question of your Shadow or any of the other subjects you've dealt with, how you approach each individual issue will be a result of the accumulation of awarenesses which you've gained through the others. Certainly, a great deal of your work in this chapter relates very directly to the chapter following this one. So, whether you begin immediately or put this aside for a few days, keep in mind the work you've just done as you move on to consider the people you have chosen as your friends.

CHAPTER 11

FRIENDSHIPS

*It is well, when one is judging a friend, to re-
member that he is judging you with the same
godlike and superior impartiality.*

ARNOLD BENNETT

In my counselling I used to find it odd and inexplicable that so
many of my clients were willing to judge their parents, their
partners, even their children with a much colder eye than
they probably deserved, but when discussion turned to their
friends, they were suddenly full of evasions. I don't mean that
they didn't complain about them. They might even spend entire
sessions thrashing out some problem they were having with them.
Nevertheless, when they had finally aired their grievances, they
seemed to assume that those friends would remain in their lives
forever, however difficult the relationship. And yet these were
often the same clients who had come to me to try to find a way
out of a long-term marriage. It was as if friends were an unalterable fact of their lives so, although they might grumble about
them, there wasn't any point in worrying too much about it.
(Their *friends* were an unalterable fact but their *families* were

not?!) In an effort to understand this, I began to examine my own friendships and was shocked to discover that I tend to act much the same way myself!

The more I thought about this whole question of friendships – how and why particular ones develop, what we get from them, give to them, why we are so loathe to alter their nature or let them go altogether – the more central the question seemed. I began to wonder, too, why it is one therapists don't focus on more routinely than they do.

Studies indicate that, once past the dating stage, men and women are likely to spend more time with their friends than they do with their families, which is not surprising when so many friendships centre around the workplace. (For the purposes of this book, 'work' includes both paid and unpaid labour and absolutely considers the raising of children and its attendant activities work.) Women particularly are apt to share their deepest fears and feelings with each other, and often to share them much more fully than they do with their partners. It should be obvious, then, that our friends exert an immensely powerful influence on us – just as we must do on them. So why don't we pay more attention to what our friends do for, and to, us? Why do we so often allow them more latitude and tolerance than we do our own families? Why are we likely to treat them with much greater patience and forbearance than we give to family members?

Above all, why don't we jettison the toxic friendships, of which nearly all of us have at least one in our lives? The excuse usually given for this is that we don't want to hurt our friends. Yet we are willing to hurt our families deeply and daily through any of the countless ways in which we let each other down in life. Is shared history alone enough to justify our holding onto a damaging friendship? Is inertia? Is fear? (All kinds of fear may enter in here – fear of loneliness, of loss of status, of what might be said behind our backs, of secrets shared which might be revealed if the friendship ended.)

Have we actually, consciously, chosen our friends or did those relationships develop by default, just because we happened to be neighbours, or to sit near each other in an office, or because *they chose us and we didn't know how to demur*? And what kind of a friend do we make? Are we ourselves the damage-makers in one or more of our friendships?

Whatever you may have got into the habit of believing about this, friends are one aspect of your life over which you *do* have a great deal of control. Even in those associations in which you feel trapped by circumstance (e.g., your partners are best friends, you have to work together, they live right next door, etc.), recognize that, although you may not have total control over the amount of time you must spend in their company, you do have absolute power over the amount of emotional investment you choose to make in that relationship.

In this section we're going to attend to the people who fill your life, absorb an enormous amount of its time and mental energy, and whom you call – perhaps accurately, perhaps not – friends. As you do these writings, be aware that this issue, especially, is one that allows for a lot of fake victimization. Try to let go of all your defences, rationalizations, and justifications –

either of your behaviour or of theirs – and ruthlessly examine why you have chosen to give these particular people so much of your life.

1. Think of the many different friendships you have had through your life and identify the one which has enriched it most completely. Don't limit this consideration only to those current or most recent friendships – you may decide that your deepest and most gratifying one was many years ago. If that is so, that's the one for you to focus on here. Write fully about this relationship, considering what it was that makes (or made) it so satisfying. What value has this person found in you which has been important to the way you value yourself? Identify those specific qualities which you received from this friendship, and those you brought to it. Is this friend still in your life? If not, why not? Have you tried to recreate those positives with other people who are in your life now? What would be necessary for you to do so?

2. This exercise will be harder than the one you've just done – and you have already anticipated it. Write as extensively and candidly as possible about a 'friend' who may be very much present in your life, but whose presence is an ongoing source of pain, discomfort or irritation to you. Do you think you *both* share this discomfort? How do you define your dissatisfaction and the reason for it? *What do you think is your contribution to this problem?* How do you think your friend would see the situation between the two of you? Have you ever discussed it with them? If yes, what was the result? If no, why not? Has

this relationship always been unsatisfactory? If not, what happened to change it? Lillian Hellman wrote, 'Well, people change and forget to tell each other. Too bad. Causes so many mistakes.' Think that over carefully. Could your difficulty be just that – that your lives have simply gone in different directions and, though fondness for your past together may remain, your friendship has run its course? Or is your difficulty with this person a long-standing, recurring one?

In either case, this is the time to analyse as comprehensively as possible your reasons for keeping this person in your life. What would you have to do to modify that? Will you? If not, why not? This is often where fake victimization comes in. Consider that as you write. Changes, even small changes, in the patterns of a lifetime are hard and, if you decide that a given relationship is one that is damaging or unsatisfactory to you, making up your mind to alter it or ease out of it altogether may be an unnerving choice. But it is your choice to make. If you act on it, you may be astounded by the relief – and the freedom – you feel as a result. If, upon reflection, you decide not to dissolve this friendship, take a cold minute to ask yourself what you are getting out of keeping it going. Peel that onion till you find the true answer.

3. Now cast your mind over the people you spend most of your time with: not necessarily the ones you like best, but the ones you actually give your time to. Write their names down and, next to each name, quickly jot down a series of words which say something important to you about your association with that person. I read somewhere that you can tell how you truly

feel about someone by your immediate visceral response on receiving a letter from them or hearing their voice on the phone. What you're after here is that same instinctive reaction to seeing their name on the page. Try not to edit this response. Again, remember that feelings are facts. No matter how uncomfortable they may be for you, those feelings are neither right nor wrong.

When you have made those notes on the half-dozen or so people who are currently consuming most of your time, write a short analysis of each of those friendships from the standpoint of benefit and loss. When you are with this person, do you feel nourished, supported, engaged, amused, challenged, etc.? If your answer to most of these is 'yes', then you already will appreciate those friendships as blessings to be treasured and nurtured.

If, as you look over your notes, there are names which you respond to with feelings of inadequacy, jealousy or irritation, or any other negative emotion, try to locate the source of those feelings. Do they result from some unacknowledged grievance or envy or hurt on your part, or on theirs? Are they perhaps arising from some unhappiness your friend is suffering from which you may not be entirely sensitive to? Or the reverse? Is there some unacknowledged competition between you which leaves your every exchange either a win or lose situation?

As you look over the names and the reactions you've written, consider what patterns you see emerging. Have you tended to make positive choices for yourself? Negative ones?

Do you look over your resulting list with pleasure?
Displeasure? If you've become aware of several relationships
which are not positive ones, evaluate how you might go about
rearranging your current priorities, making more time for the
affirmative relationships and either improving or abandoning
the negative ones.

There's a good chance that several of the names will evoke
very ambiguous feelings in you, i.e., on the one hand, they
make you laugh and provide constant entertainment, but on
the other, their humour is often unkind and leaves you feeling
uneasy after the fact. These are the associations that may call
for the closest scrutiny. Think carefully which matters most to
you – the laughter or the unease? And then look again at the
work you've just done on the question of your Shadow.

I needn't remind you that emotions are immensely fluid,
and I hope it is clear that I'm not suggesting a wholesale
clearance of people from your life just because you're going
through a rather bad patch with each other. If we can only
value each other when things are easy and pleasant between
us, it's questionable whether we really share a friendship at
all. My goal is, as always, to give you some tools to help you
recognize ways you may be keeping yourself stuck in certain
unhelpful patterns of thought or behaviour, to suggest that
you have the power to alter those those patterns, and to
encourage you to accept that that choice is *yours as well as
theirs*.

Should you decide that you want to make some alterations
in an unsatisfactory friendship, do realize that there are

several possibilities open to you – you can make peace with it, you can determine to find some way to value it, you can change its nature, or you can leave it altogether. What you decide is entirely up to you.

4. Write at length about the kind of friend you think you make. Be as frank and exacting with yourself as you can. What do you consider your greatest strengths as a friend? Your weaknesses? As you do this, try to remember what has been said to you in the past about this. What have friends told you about how they perceive you as a friend? Do their perceptions of you fit with your own? Can you identify aspects of yourself which you would like to change? Why haven't you?

   It is such an obvious truth that it is almost insulting for me to write this, but when a given hang-up is our own, it's astonishing how total our blindness to it can be. So, here goes. If, as you've done this work, your recurring conviction has been that you have been the wronged one in each difficult relationship, that you are the one who is misunderstood, that it is your friends who always let you down, there are *only* two possibilities: either you have made dreadfully punishing choices of friends, or you are not being straight with yourself. The second is almost certainly the truth. In either case, take a very hard, honest look at this issue as it might apply to you.

5. Read this knockout observation by Mark Rutherford carefully several times: 'In the presence of some people we inevitably depart from ourselves: we are inaccurate, we say things we do not feel, and talk nonsense. When we get home we are conscious that we have made fools of ourselves. Never go

near these people.' Does this have any relevance for you? If
so, what are these people doing in your life?

6. Jean Rostand wrote, 'We spend time envying people we
   wouldn't wish to be.' You may already have dealt with this
   earlier on when you were doing your first suggested writings,
   and wonder why I've included it again. Well, the reality is that
   jealousy is one emotion many of us struggle with one way or
   another all of our lives.

   Anyone who has ever experienced the feeling of jealousy
(which is everyone) recognizes it as one of the most painful
and destructive of all human emotions. It is certainly one of
the very least productive. As you write about this, keep in
mind that jealousy almost never has anything much to do with
the person who is the focus of it, but has everything to do
with your own feelings of insecurity, inadequacy and lack of
entitlement. (Or, once again, your Shadow may be lurking.)
Moreover, *it is based on two entirely fallacious assumptions*: the
first is that there is only so much of anything to go around and
if someone else possesses that thing (whatever that thing is
that you envy and desire for yourself), that other person has
somehow taken it away from you. The second is the belief that
life is a competition with only one winner. It is what
psychologists call 'operating from a scarcity model'.

   Look back over what you've written in this chapter. Can
you identify friendships in which jealousy is an element? If
not on your part, then on theirs? Write about those
friendships which seem to contain jealousy as one of their
major components. Would you honestly prefer that person's

life to yours? Think this through, with *all* of its implications, before you answer too glibly. If your conclusion is that you would not, why are you wasting your emotional energies envying them? If your answer is 'yes', then what is it exactly which they have which you think you deserve instead? Challenge yourself to discover ways your emotional energies could be spent more profitably achieving those things (or their equivalent) in your own life, instead of worrying about what other people have which you do not.

If you are aware that jealousy is something you struggle with in your life – and yet never in regard to your friends – consider whether that is due to the excellence of those friendships and your emotional generosity, or whether you only chose as friends those you feel superior to. (Please *don't*, as some are wont, decide that the latter must be the real truth because I mentioned it and it is the most negative of the two possibilities. I only ask you to *consider* the possibility, not accept it as 'fact'!)

One last, and vital point, about this entire friendship/ jealousy thing. It is an absolutely typical response of some people to approach relationships on a one-up, one-down basis. Most of us spend vastly too much of our lives trying to seem 'better than' in the terror that it will be discovered that we are actually 'worse than'. Whether your presentational mode tends towards self-deprecation or self-aggrandisement, the same ego needs are operating in both cases, and the same underlying assumptions: that love, success and happiness are finite, and can be taken from you by someone else's achievement of them. When you can accept the truth that there *is* enough to go around, that will free you to address the real issue lurking here – the way your concentration on envy and the assumed unfairness of the world allows you to duck your personal responsibility for creating your own happiness, success and love.

Blaming an unfriendly universe, or begrudging a more successful friend, can be an enormously engrossing occupation, but it will keep you permanently stuck in the fake victim role and surely by now you know that is the coward's way out, and that you deserve – and are capable of achieving – much more than that. I can almost hear you muttering as you read this, 'Well, that's rich!. That "friend" stole my partner [best mate, job, promotion, whatever]. There was only one of those to go around and they got it – not me. And it's not fair!' Perhaps. But one of the most unpalatable truths we all have to accept if we are to grow up is that life is *not* fair. Another truth is that it is only material goods which can be stolen from us. No one *owns* love or success or happiness. Since we do not own them, they cannot be stolen from us. Instead, it is our responsibility to devise creative and legitimate strategies for continually recreating those things in our lives – throughout our lives. That is a large part of what all your writing has been about.

Which leads me naturally to perhaps the most crucial element in this friendship issue. I've written about the need to forgive, and by now you've written in the attempt to do so – to parents, family members, lovers. Given that human relationships are as difficult as they are, at least some of your friendships are bound to contain some old hurts or resentments as well – either on your part or on theirs, possibly both. If you can identify such scars, for *your* sake, you must begin to try to heal them. Anger and bitterness are poisonous and soul destroying. Your holding onto those feelings may or may not damage your friend, but it is guaranteed that they will damage you. Forgiving someone not only allows you to move forward more freely with your life, but also will make it much easier for you to forgive yourself when the necessity for that arises – as it so often does.

One aspect of this friendship paradigm is worth noting here. If, over these weeks, you have actually been doing the exercises I've outlined – and if you've done them with openness and attention to the messages you've been giving yourself – you are bound to be undergoing at least some small adjustment in your attitudes, your responses and your behaviours. And as I noted early on, when one member of a group changes, the dynamics of that group will inevitably change as well. You will certainly have become aware of that truth as it concerns the people you live most closely with, but don't forget that it will also apply in your friendships. Though these shifts are positive for you, initially they may result in a rather uneasy time for the relationship. As with all dynamics of this kind, hold fast to your improved vision and ride it through. Ultimately you'll achieve a new balance with each other – this time, perhaps, one that will be more comfortable for both of you, because it will have a more authentic basis.

CHAPTER 12

DREAM WORK

We never stop seeing, perhaps that is why we dream.

GOETHE

People tend to be as fascinated by their own dreams as they are bored silly by everybody else's. Centuries before Freud, people were trying to make sense of the world their minds inhabited while their bodies were locked in sleep. In fact, there have been nearly as many theories about the meaning of dreams as there have been psychologists. Happily for all of us, I will only discuss one of these – Gestalt – the technique which I have found to have the most practical benefit. It also has this distinct advantage – you can do it entirely on your own. Trust me on this: if you are above seven years of age, no one, no matter how much they love you, wants to hear your dreams. For you as the dreamer, however, the messages you receive from them can be invaluable. Note that I said the messages *you* receive. That, to my mind, is the unique strength of this particular approach to dream interpretation. It does not depend on anyone else to interpret for you what is going on in your subconscious. You can easily develop the skills to tell yourself just what you *are* telling yourself through the metaphors of your dreams. Please stay with this. It is a powerful tool for self-awareness.

For some reason, Gestalt dream work – as a concept – is often as difficult to grasp initially as it is simple, once understood, to do. Now I don't think this difficulty results from a resistance to acknowledging subconscious truths about ourselves. It is just that, like most of the other techniques in this book, it demands a mental shift in your usual approach to thinking about things. Once you've made that shift, however, it is astonishingly easy and takes only a few moments to do.

The concept is elegantly simple. It is this: every single element in your dream is an aspect of yourself. Talk your way through each element as you think of it, *hear* what you're saying, and listen to the messages in your words.

It will be much easier if I give you an example. Let's take what psychologists normally interpret as one of the classic 'anxiety' dreams (understandably, as we all certainly tend to be anxious when we dream it). It's the one where you've shown up for an examination of some kind completely unprepared. Often you haven't just not studied, you have no idea what the exam is supposed to be about – didn't, in fact, have any idea that there was going to *be* an exam. You may not have even known that you were enrolled in the class. Generally (and this is very general indeed – as I've already said, there are countless approaches to this subject), therapists, hearing you relate this dream, will tend to encourage you to focus on what you may actually be anxious about now, in the present.

Gestaltists take a different tack. They will ask you to talk about every element in the dream as it presents itself, in the first person. Stick with me here – it will become clearer.

When doing Gestalt dream work, begin with the 'you' who appears in the dream. For instance, if I were Gestalting this exam dream for myself, I might say something like, 'I am caught. I'm not ready. I'm scared. I'm frantic. I want to run away. I'm going to fail.' Read that example over again carefully. Notice the shift here from the normal way we tend to process information. I did not describe the details of the situation – the implications or the ramifications: i.e., 'I'm sitting in this room and there's going to be a test and I haven't studied and I'm scared and upset because I know I'm going to fail and my parents will kill me and I'll probably get kicked out ... ', and so on. This is a beautiful example of how most of us remain blind to our obvious by getting bogged down in the details. Now read my first analysis of this dream again. Do you see the difference? What I have told myself is not that I'm specifically afraid of failing an exam (which is what the actual dream seemed to be about). What I must learn from this particular dream is that – at least at the time I'm analysing it – I think I am a mess, I'm a fraud, I'm scared, I'm frantic, I'm not ready, I want out, I'm a failure. Those might be my messages to myself. You will as like as not have entirely different ones. You might say, 'I am furious. I feel tricked. I'm sick of having things sprung on me.' It is even possible that your response might be, 'I'm excited. I am energized by a challenge. I'm smart enough to pull this off.' Or how about this? 'Oh God, I'm too tired. I can't face this. I want to run away.'

The point is, there will be as many possible responses as there are dreamers. All you have to do is to see yourself as you were in the dream and describe *your* emotional responses as they occur to you. Whatever you tell yourself as you do this is information for you about how you feel about yourself and your life – at least at that moment. It may be only a part of the whole picture (we're getting to a larger view – hang on!), but it's a vital part.

Do you see the power of this kind of approach? No one else is trying to tell you what you 'mean' . Which is just as well, because they can't know – because they aren't you.

Now, back to your dream. You continue this technique with each element in the dream: the books on the teacher's desk? ('I am full of knowledge. I am a valuable resource.' Or, 'I am closed. I am difficult and demanding. I am dull. I need careful attention. I think nobody wants to bother to understand me.') The desk? ('I am shabby. I have been abused. I am always used and taken for granted.' Or possibly, 'I am sturdy. I'm supportive. I am not pretty. I am useful.') What about the pencil? ('I am soft. I've been erased. I break easily.' Another possibility: 'I can create. I can show how smart I am. I can say whatever I want to.') Continue doing this with everything that appears in the dream: the window? the teacher? the exam paper? the plant on the teacher's desk? your classmates? See what I mean?

Actually, as I've just learned myself through writing this, you don't even have to have a real dream in order to do this. And in fact, if you are someone who does not remember their dreams, you might try doing what I just did – create a scenario for yourself – e.g., the exam dream – and see what comes from it. Write down any situation which occurs to you and play with the messages which emerge from your writing. Just remember to begin each sentence, 'I am …', and see what develops. Now obviously you could take this exercise to ridiculous lengths, right down to being the dust on the desk. Use your common sense, do half a dozen elements each time and let it go. Then during the day, take a minute or two occasionally to remember what you wrote down. Does it seem to have any bearing on what you're feeling now? Had you been aware that you felt that way? How can you make use of that awareness?

Freud believed that if it were possible to understand the entirety of any one dream, the whole of that individual psyche would become clear. Well, if you can do this exercise for a period of weeks, you will be amazed at how much you have learned about yourself. And I can guarantee you that much of that knowledge will astonish you.

Interestingly, it is often the most terrifying dreams, the ones which wake you with a jerk sweating, which, when treated like this, will end up giving the most positive and affirmative messages. At least, that has been true for me and many of my clients.

The difficulty, of course, is to find some way of hearing, registering and remembering what you are saying to and about yourself. This is much trickier than you suppose. Some of you may be able to solve this by telling your dreams into a tape recorder. (In this instance a recorder might be a useful tool, but even then it is only a stop-gap until you can examine later what you've learned by listening to the tape and then writing about it.) If recording does work for you, just start your stream of consciousness and begin: 'I am myself. I am___; I am the desk. I am___;' and so forth. Because I can guarantee that, unless you have some tangible way of capturing and exploring the messages of your dreams you will lose or distort them, or manage not to hear them at all. These are thoughts which you are hoping to surprise out of yourself and, as you are are catching them on the wing, they may be too fast for your fingers to capture on paper. So, if it suits you, keep a tape recorder beside your bed. Then in the morning while the dream is still fresh – and before you have time to start trying mentally to 'analyse' it – take five minutes to 'Gestalt the dream' into the recorder.

Be patient with yourself – it will probably take a bit of practice to get the knack of this mental shift. If, as you listen back to your tape, you find yourself slipping again into old habits of dealing with dreams ('… and then I noticed that the whole class had their exams papers out and I didn't have a *clue* …'), just give yourself a mental shake and begin again: 'I am …'. After a few days' practice, you'll do it without even thinking about it.

If you do not have access to a tape machine, or if using one would not ensure the privacy or non-interruption you need (or if you simply are more comfortable writing), jot down the details (no analysis, just the details of the dream) as quickly as possible when you wake and, later, when you can find time, begin to expand on the details of your notes. 'I am … .'

Whichever method you use to capture the dream initially, remember that that specific dream will only provide information about your sense of yourself *at the time* of that particular dream. The next time you do it, your mood, your self-esteem, etc., may have altered entirely. But over time, you will begin to identify general themes to the way you perceive yourself.

Because dreams come direct and unfiltered from the subconscious, the insights they offer you will be more fluid and more symbolic than those emerging from the other kinds of entries which comprise the bulk of your 'life file'. For this reason, I think it is particularly helpful if you keep your dream diary in a discrete section of your folder, separate from your other writings. This will make it much easier for you to recognize the shifting nature of your moods and self-perceptions over time.

The first great benefit to come from this sort of 'analysis' will be a growing insight into your most deeply held self-definitions, as opposed to what you may *think* those are – these may be very different from each other. Recognize this! Because the messages in your dreams come from your subconscious, they reflect the 'truths' you tell yourself about yourself and, as such, they reveal the underlying beliefs which have become the core of your self-definition. *This does not mean that they are accurate*! Much of your responsibility in this dream work is to to begin to question whether or not your dream messages are valid reflections of the way you actually live your life. One example only of this possibility: perhaps as a child you tended to be extremely disorganized. As you became aware of and dissatisfied with that trait, you worked very successfully to overcome it. For years now, you have been the first one called on to plan any ambitious project at work and/or in the community, and you have always carried it through splendidly. You, however, continue to believe that underneath your competent surface lurks the same disorganized slob you felt yourself to be as a child. Now, in your efforts to hide that 'truth' about yourself, you've organized all the spontaneity out of your life and that of your family, and it is driving them – and you – crazy. Another good illustration of personal blindness.

Another possible result of this dream work is the exact opposite. You may have decided at a young age that there were real benefits to presenting yourself as helpless or needy or inconsequential. You may have acted that role for so long that you've taught yourself to believe it. Gestalting your dreams can help you discover what a lie that is. As you sleep, you may detect a confident assurance that you don't allow yourself to manifest during the day. You might also uncover terrific anger and resentment at how easily other people dismiss you. (If so, be straight with yourself about who set up that kind of response in the first place.)

These are, of course, only hypothetical examples. But I could bet you, with absolute certainty of winning, that if you do this dream work, similar breakthroughs will happen for you.

So here we are back where we started – dream analysis is simply another weapon in your arsenal to help you 'see your obvious'. What you choose to do with your improved vision is up to you.

CHAPTER 13

ANGER

It is easy to fly into a passion – anyone can do that. But to be angry with the right person to the right extent and at the right time and with the right object and in the right way – that is not easy, and it is not everyone who can do it.

ARISTOTLE

Today's most prevalent psychological theory is that depression is anger turned inwards. My own bias is that anger is most often a mask for unexpressed, unacknowledged grief – anger is easy, grief is *hard*. Whatever the 'truth' of anger (and perhaps we're saying the same thing anyway, with just a slight difference of emphasis), anger is one of the most crucial concerns every counsellor will address with every client. It contains so many other issues within it. But it isn't actually anger itself that is the problem. It is anger which goes unacknowledged, unexpressed, or inappropriately expressed, which can't be disposed of and so stays bottled up inside with its toxins working on us – that is where the danger is.

How about you? Are you comfortable with the way you handle your anger? Are you able to express it with some control and coherence, directing it towards its legitimate source? If not, how *do* you handle your anger? Do you explode? Yell? Break things? Do you swallow it? Do you store it under pressure until it finally blows up? Does yours leak out inappropriately and indiscriminately in a frequent, generalized irritability? Do you suppress it entirely so that it can only find expression through headaches and ulcers? Do you allow yourself to show anger solely towards those people who have no power over you – and are probably not the true focus of your anger at all? Do you displace your anger and frustration with yourself onto others? The reverse? Do you only let yourself express anger through passive aggressiveness such as chronic lateness, tears, silence, or a myriad of other subtle revenges?

Let's get clear right away that I am not discussing the righteous anger which comes from a moral view of the world – anger at injustice, at unfairness, despotism, cruelty, – the etceteras here are far too long. Such anger is often the vitally necessary impetus for social change.

There are, in fact, people who displace their personal anger onto just such issues and, in doing so, effect many of the essential improvements in the world through the passionate energy and commitment fuelled by their fury. Society needs such people and we must be deeply grateful to them. However, if you are one of these it is important, for your own psychological health, to consider ways in which you can still fight for what you believe to be right without avoiding those equally legitimate sources of rage which may lie closer to home.

I will suggest that you do some writing to clarify your usual patterns around this issue, but I'll be surprised if *you* are surprised by anything much you discover. Even though we might be loathe to admit it to anyone else, this tends to be one of the few areas where we can generally see our obvious pretty clearly. The trick for most of us is not in understanding how we handle our anger, but to be aware of what its real triggers are, and to adopt more positive ways of dealing with anger when we feel it. Harder still, for some of us, is to accept that we feel it at all.

Still, you might want to reread the first couple of paragraphs of this chapter and see if you can recognize your own responses in one or more of the possibilities suggested. Then, make a mental note to yourself, identifying what you perceive to be your usual mode of expressing anger, and keep that awareness in mind as you continue your work with this issue.

It is curious that so many of us do not deal with our anger very well – particularly since it is such a natural component of being human. It is, in fact, one half of the built-in 'fight/flight' response which enables us to survive in the world.

Just as we are programmed for flight when our safety is threatened, so we are programmed to fight when we think that something we value is at risk. And therein lies much of the problem. Though it is fear that sparks our anger to begin with, for some people what should be a natural response to that threat is often swamped by an even greater fear of the consequences of expressing that anger. If experiences in your life have taught you that acceptance, approval, even love are jeopardized when you show your anger openly, it's not surprising that you find yourself frightened to let it out. And if in the past your anger was met with physical violence (or loosed your own), you have another compelling reason to be afraid of unleashing it.

But *responsible* expressions of anger are one of the most powerful channels human beings have for reaching true intimacy with each other. If your goal in any relationship is to deepen the understanding between the two of you, you have no choice but to learn to acknowledge your anger when you feel it, ascertain the correct focus of it, and risk dealing clearly and directly with that other person about it.

For your first exercise of this chapter, write a few paragraphs examining four or five different incidents in the past year in which you were aware of feeling angry. What triggered them for you? How did you handle them? What do you identify as common threads in those situations – both as to causes and responses? Do you find yourself generally upset by a sense of betrayal? Of being misunderstood? Discounted? Imposed on? Taken for granted? Identify, if you can, your common triggers. Do you consider that you resolved those difficulties satisfactorily? In each remembered instance? In some? How might you handle them differently now? Is it always basically the same kind of issue which sparks your anger? Do your responses tend always to be the same?

One typical trick many of us use is to ignore the continual mind/body interaction and thus remain unconscious of the messages our bodies are sending. We will look more closely at this particular issue in a later chapter, but for now, if you are beginning to suspect that you may not always acknowledge your anger when you feel it (or if you persist in giving it a different name), it is time to tune into your body's signals. Since anger is an atavistic fight response, adrenaline will be pumping through you at such times, whether you choose to realize it or not. One of the quickest ways I know of allowing your anger to surface is to check with your body to see what's going on. Do you feel tension in your neck and shoulders which isn't postural? A rush of blood to the head and face? A knot in your stomach? Are you smiling and calm on the surface – with clenched hands under the table?

An opposite technique, adopted by a different kind of person, is to hide behind a constant screen of excited misery – lurching from confrontation to confrontation, from crisis to crisis. This reaction usually involves lots of yelling and physical activity: it may even include violence. On the surface, these two adaptations seem entirely dissimilar, but they actually achieve exactly the same result – they establish an almost impenetrable barrier between that person and the target of their anger. If your pattern is either to pretend nothing's wrong at all, or to huff and puff and blow the other person's house down, this is an issue for you to work on.

One reason this is such a tricky subject to deal with is that anger must have as its focus another person – one who is usually important to us in one way or another, and one who will be bringing their own emotional baggage to this potential confrontation. (The rage we all feel occasionally towards inanimate objects or an uncaring fate is frustration, not anger – and it is a fact of life. You can and should develop coping mechanisms for such moments but, unlike true anger, the only help for such times is perspective and a sense of humour. Though, come to think of it, perspective and humour are pretty powerful supports when you're mad at someone, too.)

I'm going to make another statement of the obvious here, and I encourage you not to dismiss it impatiently as too self-evident to merit attention: *the one who cares the least has the power.* Notice that I did not say that the one who yells the loudest, or threatens the most, or seems the most assured, or argues the most convincingly, or even the one who hits the hardest; *I said the one who cares the least.* Power and control fears are often at the core of our anger and some people are very likely to assume that they don't have enough of either. But take a moment now, when you are not in the midst of an argument, to consider what implications that truth might have for some of your most important relationships. How might the awareness that you might actually be the one in the power seat affect your response and/or behaviour the next time a conflict arises?

So. You have accepted that you are legitimately angry. Your body is telling you that and so is your mind. You have even decided that you are clear about the precise object of your anger. Regardless of who holds the power, you care enough about this issue to fight for it. Now what? Try (and this is never easy) taking a deep breath and, instead of counting to 10, use those seconds before reacting to check your interpretation of the words or behaviour that lit your fuse. Is it possible that you misinterpreted or prejudged the words or event? Are you angry because you expected the other person to read your mind about something and they failed to do so? Disappointed because the other person has just indicated you are not going to receive something you feel entitled to? Did they know you thought you were? Are you really still mad about something else entirely that happened between you two long ago and which you've been afraid to face? (This quick breath is not for the purpose of allowing you to discount the anger you feel, it's intended to aid you in expressing that feeling as clearly as possible.) Obviously you needn't mentally run through every possible scenario before responding, but the mind does work at lightning speed and the amount of processing it can do in brief seconds is astonishing. Remember the actor's tricks here and watch your timing. If you allow yourself to rush into either verbal assault or self-defence right away, it may feel good for a second, but the whole situation is bound to escalate beyond all reason and it is almost guaranteed that there will be no satisfactory resolution for either person involved.

It is nearly impossible to be faced with someone else's anger without feeling either attacked or challenged. That is where this whole issue gets so difficult. You may or may not be objectively 'right' about your feelings at this moment, but if you express them carelessly and accusatorially, your adversary (at least at this moment) is almost guaranteed to don their armour of defences and you've both lost.

I'm afraid this is the time for you to use those 'I' messages people make such fun of when they're ridiculing psychological evangelists. The fact is, if you launch into an attack with something that includes name calling, and statements which contain phrases like, 'You always ... ', or 'You never ... ', you're both sunk. And if those outbreaks are accompanied by screaming and/or uncontrollable sobs, you're double sunk, double fast.

I am not suggesting that you try to explain your feelings without showing any emotion at all. I am only urging you to admit that they are *your* feelings and to take responsibility for them. For instance, it is helpful to be able to frame your statement in this manner: 'When you say [or do] ... , *I* feel angry because *I* want [or feel, or expect, or believe] ... .'

Examples like that always make me uneasy, because they sound so rational and contrived just when I'm feeling my most frenzied and real. Nevertheless, contained within that example are the three guidelines for fighting with some chance of getting more out of it than carnage.

1. Own the anger as yours. '*I* feel mad', *not* '*You* make me mad when ....' And no fudging the issue with '*It* makes me mad when ....' It's your anger you're dealing with here, no one imposed it on you from the outside. Furthermore, it is a legitimate emotion and you have every right to feel it, even if it turns out later you misread the situation. Respect yourself enough to take responsibility for your authentic feelings.

2. Now respect your relationship enough to explain *precisely* what words or behaviours have triggered that angry response from you. Do not expect the other person to know your reasons through telepathy, or to be able to guess, or to understand you so well that they should automatically comprehend what's bugging you. Provide specific examples. Specific examples from *this* specific situation. This is not the moment to drag up all the other times you were furious with their behaviour. Save that till you've both calmed down and the atmosphere is more conducive to hearing each other out clearly.

3. This is perhaps the most important step of all: explain as
   rationally and honestly as possible, what it was that you
   perceived behind their words or behaviours that spurred your
   anger. For example, 'When you interrupt me, I get furious
   because I feel you think what I'm saying is so unimportant
   you don't even need to listen to it – and, anyway, I'm so
   predictable you already know what's coming.'

If your true agenda is to bring the house down around your ears,
face that, accept it, and try to arrange that demolition with as little devastation to both of you as possible. If your anger is really
just an accumulation of built-up frustrations with life in general
and you want a good slanging match to let off steam, recognize
that and hit pillows, or tennis balls, or go for a good long walk,
but keep it *your* problem. Which it is.

But if this is a relationship which truly matters to you, value it
– and yourself – enough to risk your anger when you feel it and
express it in a way that might bring the two of you closer than you
dreamed was possible. It's your right – and your responsibility –
to *ask* for what you need, and to be clear about the way you expect to be treated. But if you haven't asked, openly and plainly, it
is irrational to be angry if you don't get it.

The following was number 28 of the 30 writing topics suggested
at the beginning of the book. If it is one you wrote about at the
time, take another look at it now in light of the points discussed
in this chapter. If you did not choose to write on this at the time,
why not do so now? 'Write about the angriest you can ever

remember being. What triggered it? How did you handle it? Was it with someone else or with yourself? Are you still angry about it? If yes, what is that anger doing to, or for, you? If no, how did you resolve it? Is either behaviour a pattern you've used through your life?'

The next time you feel suffused with anger, try to follow the three guidelines I suggested, recognizing that you'll get better at it with practice. Remember, habit is overcome by habit.

CHAPTER 14

FACING FEARS

*It is not because things are difficult that we do
not dare; it is because we do not dare that they
are difficult.*

SENECA

Since I've just finished defining fear as a natural response to
life's dangers – a response vital for the activation of our
fight/flight survival mechanism, it may seem strange that
I'm getting ready to devote an entire chapter to it. The thing is,
most of us are apt to find it very difficult to tell the difference between what is an appropriate reaction to an actual threat, and the
phony, completely subjective fears we manufacture for ourselves
as yet another unhappy technique for keeping ourselves stuck in
old habits.

If you are being chased by a tiger, you either use any method
you can think of to immobilize that tiger, or you run like the
devil. (Let's assume, for the purposes of this illustration, that you
aren't so hypnotized that you just stand there and get eaten.) It is
a straightforward action/reaction. You have identified a legitimate
threat and have acted constructively to save yourself from it.

However terrified you may have been, you have resolved the situation.

Our neurotic behaviour is not so simple of course. It's not that we can't respond appropriately to valid dangers when they present themselves, it's just that we seem to feel the need to go one step further and imagine (or overestimate) risks where none may exist, at least not to the degree we choose to believe. We can be real masters at creating bogus perils for ourselves – they supply such splendid excuses for avoiding all kinds of engagements with life.

Imagine that someone with a healthy ego becomes aware of an irrational fear that limits them from doing something they would like to do. Their solution is to devise practical strategies for over-coming that apprehension. If, for example, they have a fear of flying, they might combat it by taking flying lessons, or by learn-ing as much as possible about the principles of aerodynamics, or by taking as many flights as possible to extinguish their anxiety. Whatever method they use, they are willing to name their fear, *challenge the validity of it*, and then find some way of tackling it.

In similar circumstances, the neurotic's response is likely to be, 'Oh well, I never really wanted to go to Rio, anyway. Besides, I hear Cleveland is lovely in mid-winter.' Neat. But this person has not only given up the chance to experience Rio, but they have also avoided the opportunity to experience new adventures in a strange setting where the language and mores will be unfamiliar to them. Or was that their real concern all along?

Now there are two important issues hiding behind the obvious of that last paragraph, and each contains vital information for us. First, phony fears always mask something we both desire *and* dread. If we don't secretly (i.e., secret from ourselves) want to do something, we simply don't do it – we do not bother fearing it. Please don't ignore this truth by coming up with silly examples to make nonsense of it. Bungee jumping may or may not be a ridiculously dangerous pursuit, but obviously you don't *necessarily* have to have a secret yen to do it to find it so. Let's take a more sensible example which is likely to be closer to home. If you have been very much hurt in a past relationship, it is not unlikely that you might have devised a whole scenario of disasters to 'protect' yourself from the dangers of entering into another relationship, even though you want terribly to share your life with someone. But if you concentrate only on the potential risks, you will never find out if those risks were only hypothetical or real, will you?

Or here's another example: you've always been interested in local politics and feel you have much to contribute to the community, but you wouldn't even consider standing for office because you are terrified of public speaking. That is your *admitted* fear – the deeper concern which underlies it is that you might stand and lose, and then be exposed as both a poor orator and a loser.

You see? Your fears achieve several unhealthy objectives in those examples. They both mask your unadmitted desire and then allow you to avoid ever having to test the validity of your fears. Since your fears give you an excuse not to try, you'll never fail. But you'll never have a chance to succeed, either. So here's the second lesson, and it is one that you ignore at your peril: when you allow fear to deter you from a risk worth taking, a risk you *want* to take, you are not protecting yourself, you are only protecting your fear and keeping it alive. Let me say that again: every time you do not face your fear, you feed it, guaranteeing that it will return later, hungrier than ever.

The single common factor underlying most of our fears is the loss of control. We invariably struggle with control issues (more on this later in Chapter 17), either ceding way too much control to others or trying to grab too much for ourselves. That earlier example about the fear of flying is a perfect example of this. We all know the statistics about the safety of flight compared to the safety of driving. In spite of those facts, and in spite of the reality that pilots are trained, tested and experienced (far beyond whatever skills we may bring to our driving), most people will admit to at least some nervousness about flying. That's because we all operate under the myth of control – and at 30,000 feet we are forced to accept that we have none. One of the greatest leaps you can make towards sound health is to realize that, at best, you can only control certain aspects of *yourself*. You certainly cannot control life or the other people involved in it with you. Life – and love – *are* risk. But since the underlying aim of most of our bad habits of behaviour is the achievement of control and the avoidance of risk, we are continually setting ourselves up for failure.

Control is illusory and life is a gamble. Those are non-negotiable facts. And when you can accept that reality for yourself, you can begin to pay attention to the ways you have tried to achieve the unachievable, and look instead for new methods of engagement rather than old methods of avoidance. Like everything else, it will get easier with practice. And you'll get braver with experience.

Remember (in Chapter 8) my quoting the Gestalt psychologist Fritz Perls' assertion that, when you are afraid, all you have to do is to take a deep breath and let yourself feel the excitement which that fear is masking? Keep that observation in mind the next time you are faced with a situation which fills you with apprehension. Then try taking that deep, deep breath and let yourself experiment with the chance that Perls might just be right. How would accepting that your fear is actually a cover for your excitement change your way of dealing with that situation?

Let me tell you the true story of a friend of mine. He is a man who was widowed in early middle age following some years of a not terribly happy marriage. In fact, he and his wife had begun marriage counselling before she became ill. When she died, he started seeing the counsellor again, hoping to resolve some of the painful ambiguities which he still felt about their marriage and her death. In one of their sessions he said that he felt trapped by the 'suffering victim' image people tended to ascribe to him as a bereaved widower. He did grieve for his wife, but he was also fully aware of what had been the inadequacies of their marriage. He was frightened to reveal this truth to anyone in case their compassionate sympathy turned instead to contempt for what (he was sure) they would regard as a callous lack of feeling. His counsellor dared him to test out the validity of this fear by telling at least one person the truth. He left his appointment that day, determined to act on that suggestion before he could lose his nerve. Stopping at a restaurant on his way home, he ran into a woman he had only met a few times socially. After the briefest of greetings, he blurted out, rather desperately, 'I was only moderately happy in my marriage!' That was nine years ago and he and that woman have now been married – very happily – for eight of those nine years. Isn't that a marvellous story? And can you imagine how difficult it must have been for him to do what he did?

Look for a moment at what happened there. He accepted both his fear (that he would be judged harshly and rejected if his true feelings were revealed), and its underlying desire (that someone could understand and accept those feelings without finding them reprehensible). Then he found the courage to take what seemed to him to be an enormous risk – to let go of all his defences and be completely honest with another human being. Well, isn't that the same challenge we all face? What would it require for you to take a similar gamble yourself?

1. Write about two or three fears which you are aware of in yourself, and try to find in them the desire you might be hiding from yourself. When that is done, consider what is the worst that could happen if you overcame your anxiety, confronted your fear and tried to achieve that desire? If the worst did happen, would you die? Have a nervous breakdown? Would it destroy your life? Cause irrevocable damage to people you love? If the honest answer is 'no' to all of those questions, try experimenting on paper with how you might handle it if your risk didn't pay off. *What do you get out of protecting your fear and keeping it alive?* Is that pay-off more valuable to you than the rewards you might gain if you confronted your fears, defied them, and won? Really spend some time working on and thinking about this.

2. Write about those same fears you've identified above, imagining that you've had the courage to face and fight them. What did you discover about yourself and about the legitimacy of your phony fears in doing so? Could you find the nerve to do some reality testing with at least one of them, and see what might develop?
3. Remember my friend's story. Would you be willing to identify the hardest thing you can imagine doing – and then to do it?

CHAPTER 15

WHATEVER BECAME OF SIN?

True guilt is guilt at the obligation one owes to oneself to be oneself. False guilt is guilt felt at not being what other people feel one ought to be or assume that one is.

R. D. LAING

The insights of psychology have done much to help us to understand and forgive ourselves for some of our less admirable behaviours, and this can only be a benefit. But it sometimes seems to me that one unintended consequence of our improved understanding has been an accompanying loss of moral content in our lives. And I think we damage ourselves if we use 'psychology' to try to let ourselves off the moral hook. Or, as Peg Bracken wryly sums up the current attitude, 'It's 50% heredity and 50% environment, so it's not my fault!'

In this chapter I would like to make a serious case for the need to recognize the sins we commit and the appropriate guilt which results from the commission of them. Then we will consider the neurotic, false guilt which we use to keep us immobilized.

It is necessary to walk a rather schizophrenic path in our lives today. On the one hand, most of us have quite a number of people in our lives who seem to encourage us to feel guilty for the ways they consider we have failed to live up to *their* expectations. On the other hand, there is a constant flow of psychiatrists on radio and television offering explanations (which can sound very like excuses) for our destructive behaviours. If we have been scarred by life (and who hasn't?), somehow that seems to absolve us of all responsibility for our actions. Except that it doesn't. At some profound level, we ourselves are damaged if we don't confront our culpability and make some kind of amendment.

Read Laing's statement at the beginning of this chapter again, and pay attention to its implications – they hold the key to separating appropriate guilt from false guilt.

True guilt always results from any behaviour which is in violation of your own most deeply held values and beliefs. Please notice that I said *your* values and beliefs. Since you are only neurotic, not crazy, you will automatically judge all of your actions in the light of your *own* visceral sense of right and wrong – 'the obligation one owes to oneself to be [true to] oneself'. It is not up to me as a counsellor to evaluate your personal value system – nor is it up to anyone else. But when we transgress against our *own* ethics, ultimately we ourselves will suffer more deeply than those we have injured. Remember Elmer Hubbard's observation that 'Men are not punished for their sins, but by them.'

The Bible reminds us that none is without sin. Since it is unlikely that you are the sole exception to that, why not pull out your writing materials now and take some time to identify occasions in your life when your desires conflicted with your ethics and your desires won. Can you distinguish one (or several) time(s) when you may have 'got away with it' as far as the world is concerned, but you yourself are still aware of feeling ashamed? We must all learn to forgive ourselves over and over again if we are to be able to get up in the mornings, but you will not truly be able to do so until you admit your guilt to yourself and find some way of rectifying whatever damage you caused – or intended. I don't pretend that this will be easy, nor do I pretend that you will necessarily find forgiveness from those you have wronged. But I do say that, for *your* sake, it must be attempted.

It is possible that you are haunted by the memory of some transgression against a person no longer living. If that is the case, I urge you to write through that situation as completely as possible – and then find some way you can repay 'in kind' somewhere else in your life. Much that we have done cannot be undone: we are all haunted by that truth throughout our lives. But a sincere attempt at rectification can do a great deal to begin *your* healing.

Now turn to the second part of Laing's statement: 'False guilt is guilt felt at not being what other people feel one ought to be or assume that one is.' For most of us this is likely to be the real whammy in this issue of guilt. It is almost a definition of neurosis to say that you are likely to have lived your life either bowing to or rebelling against others' expectations of you. And since those expectations are unlikely to be a perfect fit, you are bound, continually, to 'fail' to meet them.

Enter false guilt. False guilt is the response of the 'naughty child' within us – and its concomitant is the fear of every child – that their 'naughty' behaviour will result in punishment, deep disapproval or the withdrawal of affection. Unlike appropriate guilt, which can be accepted, confronted and, at least to some extent, expiated, there can be no satisfactory resolution to false guilt because it is the consequence of failing to meet *someone else's* values, not your own.

As painful and debilitating as false guilt is, it is also a powerful weapon in the neurotic's arsenal – a splendidly effective tool for keeping us stuck. Just as false fear is a mask for an unacknowledged desire, so false guilt is a mask for some other emotion we are unwilling to face.

Can you identify a situation or a relationship in which you have avoided confrontation or self-assertion for fear that the other person involved will be angry with you or reject you? Ask yourself whether you might have convinced yourself that your lack of action was appropriate because you had been wrong to feel or desire those things in the first place? (Implicit in that is the learned belief that it isn't 'nice' to make a fuss.) If so, the next step is obvious; you feel 'guilty' about your feelings and blame yourself for having had them.

Isn't that a truly elegant dynamic? Just look at all the things we manage to accomplish with it: we discount our right to – and our responsibility for – our authentic feelings and desires; we avoid facing our fears and by so doing keep them alive; we deny to ourselves that what we are really avoiding is the possibility that the other person either cannot (or may not choose to) accept us as we are or give us what we need; we cede power to the other person by anticipating their response and according their needs greater validity than our own; and finally, since false guilt virtually *precludes* action, we don't have to do anything about it. Most of all, we don't have to acknowledge the true emotion which is hidden behind that guilt – a deep and self-punishing anger. Anger both with that other person *and*, at some level, anger with ourselves for indulging in such avoidance. *False guilt is very often anger which we have turned in on ourselves.*

The anger you feel (which is here masquerading as guilt) is not just at the other person (for not giving you what you need without you having to ask for it), but at yourself as well (for not valuing yourself enough to ask for what you need). You will only be able to shed this kind of pattern by confronting both of those truths.

Another favourite gambit is to accept phony guilt as a way of avoiding responsibility for a true fault. As I've already said, false guilt tends to make action – and therefore resolution – virtually impossible. (Though, perversely, some people often seem to assume that just feeling guilty confirms in them a kind of virtue – as if simply experiencing guilt is enough to restore probity. Another elegant con for avoiding responsibility.)

To use an example which may not be as trivial as it at first seems, let's suppose that someone has done you an unexpected and unsolicited kindness – one which came at a time when you were particularly in need of it. Though at the time you may have said a quick, even heartfelt 'thank you', you are nagged by the sense that you 'should' have followed that verbal acknowledgement with a note or some more concrete expression of appreciation. After all, you were taught to always send thank you letters. Now you feel that you've let it go too long and there's no point. Still, you continue to feel guilty whenever you see or think about that person.

By labelling your 'guilt' as a failure of manners, you are not acknowledging the more serious omission which is at the heart of it. Someone reached out to you in good will, perhaps even in compassion, and you recognize that your response was too casual, too social to reflect your deepest feelings of gratitude. It is not a matter of needing to send a bread-and-butter note, but of *your* necessity to express the profound importance to you of that other person's generosity. You are not guilty of insufficient graciousness but of insufficient humanity. As long as you are both breathing, it is *never* too late to reach back to someone who has touched you. (What are 'manners' anyway, if not the demonstration of your understanding that other people have feelings too?)

I've tried very hard to avoid using the buzz words of popular psychology in this book, but there is one categorization that I do find useful when dealing with clients – the 'tyranny of the shoulds' – that shorthand label for all of those standards and values which are constantly being imposed on us by others. It is not that there is *necessarily* anything wrong with them in themselves. It is just that, first, they may not be right for us personally and, second, being told that someone else knows better than we do is always enraging. It gets in the way of our figuring things out for ourselves. Paradoxically, sometimes our need to rebel against those 'shoulds' leads us away from doing what we ourselves had already determined was right. Other people's 'shoulds' account for a tremendous amount of the emotional baggage we all are worn out from carrying. And they are the basis for much of our mental pain and false guilt.

Again, your body can really help you here. The next time someone starts to tell you what you 'should' do, do an immediate body check. Consciously screen your body's response to the instruction you've just been given. Does that 'should' feel comfortable? How does your body feel if you change that 'should' to a choice *you* make for yourself, 'I choose to ...'? And, if you give yourself even more leeway: 'I will, sometime, when ...'? At each step of this process monitor your body for the truth of what you are telling yourself. If it is difficult for you to accept this 'should' under any circumstances, examine your reasons for this before discarding the directive out of hand. Remember, your goal is never to allow someone else's agenda to drive you. It is not to cut off your nose to spite your face – or theirs. But if, after a full assessment, you still feel that that 'should' does not belong in your life, let go of it, and let go of the unhealthy guilt which may result if you don't.

This subject of false guilt can be a particularly fertile field for digging up and weeding out some of those learned but now out-grown habits of attitude and belief that no longer have any validity. If you do become aware of some of these old messages, this is the time to challenge them and consciously begin trans-planting your own values into their place.

Your job then, for the work of this chapter, is to examine those areas in your life in which you are aware of feelings of shame. As you write about them, determine whether that shame is a legiti-mate response to a transgression (of commission or omission). If your conscience confirms your fault, devise a plan for making whatever amends you can, and then, *follow that plan through*.

If, on the other hand, you recognize your overriding uneasiness as an instance of false guilt, write about that, considering just whose values have been driving you, and just how you can go about getting free of their 'shoulds' so that your own can be heard.

One of the writing suggestions at the very beginning of this book was this: 'Simone Weil said, "All sins are attempts to fill voids." Think about this as you consider what voids you are trying to fill – and the sins you resort to to do so.' If this was an exercise you chose at the time, find that essay now and reread it. Anything you want to add – or subtract? If you have not used this insight as a basis for self-examination, why don't you do so now?

CHAPTER 16

HONOUR YOUR INSTINCTS

Penetrating so many secrets, we cease to believe in the unknowable. But there it sits neverthe-less, calmly licking its chops.

MENKEN

In the first chapter of this book I talked about the great diffi-culty most of us face in trying to trust, trying even to *recognize*, our instincts – hidden as they tend to be under so much of the emotional garbage which we, and others, and life have piled on top of them. And yet, it is our instincts, our gut feel-ings, which should be our truest and most reliable source for self-understanding.

In this chapter your task will be to learn how to be alive to the messages your body is continually sending to you (and to others) – messages which you may be oblivious to.

I've already touched on this in several previous chapters, but it is important for you to remember that this mind/body connection is *always* at work – not just in moments of stress – sending sig-nals which are full of vital information for you. Now that may seem like yet another patronizing statement of the all-too-evident, but many of us are apt to remain completely cut off from what our bodies are telling us. It is just another way we remain impervious to our obvious. Even those who attend to their bodies relentlessly with exercise and diet regimes are likely to do so more as if their bodies were machines in need of constant tuning rather than as conduits to the unconscious.

We are human *animals*, and we share with the other members of the animal kingdom the very same instincts and autonomic responses which determine their behaviour – and their survival. The problem is that, unlike our animal cousins, our minds often get in the way of our attentiveness to those internal cues. Well, everything in life is a trade-off, and one questionable trade-off human beings have made is an over-reliance on the brain and an under-reliance on the body as an instrument for awareness. But the combination of the two, working together, is unbeatable.

Our bodies are continually mirroring every emotion that we are experiencing. Voice, shoulders, head, hands, stomach, even toes – each is providing us with information at every moment of our lives. And we do receive that information, but all too often we receive it only on the subconscious level. Further, unlike other animals, we are dangerously prone to ignore or misinterpret the warnings we are getting, even when we are conscious of them.

Several times clients of mine would proclaim proudly, 'I always trust my instincts. They haven't let me down yet.' This, in spite of the fact that they had come for counselling because they felt that their lives were falling apart. It is certainly crucial for you to learn to trust your instincts, but you can only afford to do so when you have clear access to them – and can challenge their validity. For most of us, what we call instinct is often no more than a reaction to what we perceive or desire, however wrongly driven those perceptions and desires might be.

There is one essential caveat to keep in mind here. Your body is your purest information centre, continually processing and feeding back to you information about yourself and your most visceral responses. Which does *not* mean that that information is an *accurate* reflection of an outward reality. Just as a dog which has been beaten will continue to cower when it sees a raised hand (even if that hand was only raised to wave at a passer-by), your body has been programmed by the learned expectations and experiences of your past. It is highly likely that at least some of the messages you are receiving are no longer applicable to the person you have become or the life you are now living. But, as I may have said too often by now, unless you learn to recognize the assumptions which drive you, you cannot question them and begin to reprogramme yourself, body *and* mind, to process your experiences in the light of your current reality.

So your challenge in this chapter – and for the rest of your life – is to become attuned to what your body is telling you about your most authentic responses to the situations and relationships in your life. All of the exercises you have done until now were devised to help you to see yourself more clearly, to know yourself more profoundly and to achieve some congruity between the self you desire to be, the self you believe yourself to be, and the self you present to the world. Your greatest ally in this struggle will be your increasing awareness of your body's automatic reactions to the various stimuli of your life. Just remember to respect the information you are receiving, while continuing to do a reality check about its current validity.

If you've done the work of the previous chapters truthfully and openly, you are learning to identify the authentic sources of your various emotions as you feel them, and you are getting much more accomplished in your ability to assign accurate labels to them. The only thing necessary now is to try to broaden the scope of your attention, staying alert to your physical reactions, even at moments which you do not consider to be stressful.

How do you generally carry yourself? Does your posture tend towards rigidity? Do you slump? Where do you tend to carry your tension? In your throat? Your shoulders? Your back? Your neck? What is your habitual expression? Do you frown more than you had realized? Look impatient? Bored? What about your voice? Your voice provides particularly vivid indications of your internal state, if you'll just listen to it. Is yours shrill? Strangulated? Harsh? Expressionless? Whiny? Childish? Do you mumble so that people are constantly asking you to repeat yourself? Do you tend to use your voice as a weapon?

If you attend to these clues, the possibilities for insight are enormous, as are the possibilities for deciding just what those things 'mean' to you psychologically. Once again, it is not up to me or anyone else to assign a psychological significance to your physical manifestations. But you will probably begin to do that for yourself as you become increasingly tuned into them. At that point, it's up to you to decide what alterations, if any, you choose to make.

One tip: this is a particularly easy and fruitful area for exercising the 'as if' option. Here is only one of many possible examples:

if you have become aware that your body is tense by habit rather than in response to a particular stress, or if you find yourself frowning without any reason to, make a conscious effort to relax the muscles in your body and/or face. Not only will you be doing your body a favour, but the odds are you'll feel a surprising improvement in your mood as well. Your body is just as likely as your mind to suffer from old habits which are no longer appropriate for you.

I have often referred to the ideal of achieving a congruence of belief and reality. As you are likely to have discovered through your writings, there can be quite a disparity between what you *think* you feel and what you, in fact, *do* feel. During those times when your life is especially out of kilter, this gap can become alarmingly wide. People are often aware that they swallow or disown their painful feelings. But I have had clients so numbed in general that they didn't even recognize *pleasure* when they felt it. Learn to check with your body for the truth of your perceptions.

For instance, you believe that you are quite comfortable in a given situation. Do your shoulders seem to reflect that comfort? Does your voice? Your stomach? Or perhaps you have a friend with whom you spend a lot of enjoyable time, and yet often you find yourself returning home afterwards with a mild headache. Assuming that that time together didn't include alcohol, what's going on within you or between the two of you which might account for the headache? Or maybe alcohol did play a part and that is the basis for your friendship. Is it possible that it is the drinking which keeps this friendship alive and, at a deeper level, you are aware of that and are uneasy about it? The next time you and this person are together, tune into whatever signals your body may be sending you and see what sense you can make of the emotional hangovers you are experiencing.

Or, on a more positive note, and remembering that fear is often repressed excitement, can you become sensitive enough to your body's signs to recognize the difference between the two? The distinctions between fear and excitement may be subtle but they do exist and you can learn to read them, and to respond accordingly.

We like to think that we are fooling other people when the only person we are really fooling is ourselves. Let me give you an example of how this manifested itself with a woman I know. Divorced for several years, she spoke openly of her desire to form another relationship and frequently mourned the dearth of attractive, available men. One day we were in a restaurant having lunch together when a man who was not only available and attractive, but also obviously interested in her, stopped by our table to talk. Now, one of the gestures characteristic of this woman is to hold her hands shoulder high, close to her body, palms facing outward. Well, the minute this man appeared, though she smiled and chatted pleasantly with him, this gesture broadened so that her arm now shot straight out in front of her in the policeman's 'STOP' signal. She may not have been aware of the message she was sending, but he certainly received it, loud and clear.

When I mentioned this to her after he had gone (looking both puzzled and disappointed), she was astonished. Her perception was that she had been almost pathetically flirtatious with him. We chewed this over for some time before she came to the rather rueful conclusion that she was clearly still a great deal more skittish and frightened than she had had any idea of. She decided that she might need to do a little more healing before she was ready to make herself vulnerable again romantically. Her body had certainly recognized this – her mind was still slow in catching on. She left that day determined to sort out for herself which was the truer perception. She decided that this was a great opportunity to discover whether her subconscious (manifest in her 'stop' sign) was providing her with a valuable warning or was simply stuck in the groove of a worn out self-protection record she would do better to discard.

Can you find any correlations for this kind of dynamic in some of your own interactions? Is your body signalling what you think it is? What you hope it is? If not, what is really going on inside you?

Begin to pay attention to the gestures you use in your dealings with other people. How often have you thought you were open and receptive to someone else's point of view, when your body was telling quite a different story (easily interpreted by the on-looker) through the arms you were hugging tightly crossed against your chest? Have you ever believed that you were making your case coolly and objectively only to realize later that during the entire time you had been leaning towards the other person in a physical posture of supplication?

Are you aware that touching can be a power signal and that the one who touches first is attempting to assert theirs? Is it possible that, at least sometimes, when you touch you are not expressing the affection you assumed, but are instead trying to get control of the other person or the situation? (If you decide that you do sometimes use touch for power, you need not recoil from that awareness. There is nothing inherently wrong with such a manoeuvre. Just file that knowledge away and teach yourself to recognize the difference of agenda in each case.)

The possibilities are so vast that I could go on suggesting hypothetical variations on this theme for hundreds of pages, but you've got the idea already. Your obvious next step is to become increasingly vigilant in the attention you pay to the signals your body is sending, and equally heedful of the messages you will be receiving from them.

And (here we go again!), even if it feels artificial at first, practise presenting yourself in a way that is compatible with the way you want to be perceived. Remember, ballet dancers train their bodies to do the most unnatural things and are able to assume postures which somehow seem both beautiful and inevitable when they are performed. With time and practice, your created presence will have the same effect of rightness and inevitability for you.

A quick addendum to all of this, and yet another statement of what should be obvious. It is your responsibility to attend to your physical as well as your emotional health. If you are aware of a constant headache, a knot in your stomach or any other constant physical symptom, don't, for *your* sake, take the coward's way out. Do *not* just write it off as a symptom of emotional distress. Do not convince yourself that if you just ignore it, it will go away. Get yourself to the doctor for a thorough physical examination. Then, when you've been given a clean bill of health, you'll be able to listen to your body without your anxieties deafening you to it.

Your work for this chapter involves borrowing one last trick from the actor's repertoire – a technique called sense memory. Have you ever wondered at an actor's ability to cry real tears, night after night, on cue? Sometimes, of course, he or she may actually be so alive to the truth of the moment that the tears follow naturally from the events on stage. But even the most dedicated Method actors find this kind of immediacy nearly impossible to pull off eight performances a week. That's where their training in sense memory comes in. And I stress the word 'training'. This exercise may seem difficult for you at first, but you are just as capable as any actor of training your own imagination and memory to help you increase your sensitivity to the messages your body is sending.

Let me expand on that example of the actor whose role demands tears at every performance. He or she has learned to trick the body into a physical response (in this case, tears), not by immersing him or herself in the emotions of the character being portrayed at that moment, but by accessing a specific, painful memory from the past of his or her own life. You can learn to do this too. You too can train your memory to be a conduit to your body.

Try this. Sit quietly – with your writing materials – close your eyes and imagine yourself back into an episode in your life which had powerful emotional resonance for you. A disagreement with a child? A conversation with a parent? Some event at work? The possibility of some change in your life? A romantic meeting? Whatever situation you choose, try to recreate it as fully and as vividly as you can. See yourself in that setting. Feel yourself there.

See and feel whoever else was present with you at that moment. Warm your way into this memory by reliving whatever sense of cold or heat might have been part of the scene, any particular smells or sounds. As the images become increasingly intense, try to keep one small inner sensor alert to whatever physical responses may be occurring within you.

Only when you have allowed your imagination (as opposed to your conscious mind) full play, and *only* then, turn to your writing materials and note quickly whatever you can identify about what your body might be telling you.

Is there tension? Where do you feel it? Or perhaps a sense of release? Tears or the feeling of being on the edge of tears? Maybe you feel a smile trembling on your lips? Are you shivering? Do you feel fear? Excitement? Anger? Hurt? Frustration? Joy? Elation? Whatever words you have jotted down, consider carefully now whether you have labelled them accurately. Could what you've labelled 'happiness' more truly be called triumph? Are you sure that your 'hurt' is not actually unacknowledged resentment, or vice versa? With each challenge to yourself for the truth of your feelings, check with your body. What is it saying?

Dig a little deeper now. Does it seem that the physical sensations you're aware of in yourself now reflect accurately whatever meanings you ascribed to that incident at the time it happened? Can you get in touch with other responses which you may not have recognized when the actual event was occurring? Is there any important new information which your instincts are signalling you about? Examine now, through your writing, any insights which may have come to you from this sense memory exercise – with the promise to yourself that you will repeat such imaging whenever you feel it might be helpful to sort out an encounter which has left you feeling confused, or off-balance, or obscurely unsettled.

CHAPTER 17

BOUNDARIES

I am I and you are you and I am not in this
world to live up to your expectations.

GESTALT PRAYER

The first intimation we have that life may turn out to be trickier than we had assumed occurs when, as children, we start to realize that we are actually separate beings from our mothers. At that moment we begin the struggle which will determine most of the satisfactions we will find in the adulthood which lies ahead for us – the struggle to establish comfortable limits to that separateness from all other human beings. This undertaking becomes particularly acute when we reach adolescence, which helps to explain why (in addition to all the chaotic hormonal activity going on), those years can be almost unbearably rocky; not only for ourselves but for all those others who must deal with us. But if we can achieve a reasonable autonomy during that time, and if we can learn to set workable boundaries for ourselves, we will come to adulthood well prepared to deal with its challenges.

Most of us reach adulthood grown but less prepared than we had anticipated. Still, this task is inescapable. If you do not accomplish your necessary growth work at the stage appropriate for it, you'll have to attend to it later in life if you plan to live as fully and richly as possible. That is what this chapter is about.

Until you learn to erect suitable boundaries, all of your important relationships will continue to be characterized either by an unhealthy enmeshment or an equally unhealthy distance. Paradoxically, true intimacy is only possible when it is restrained by limits. When two autonomous, self-realized egos come together by free choice, a remarkable oneness is allowed to develop. But when two people, driven by their need to absorb or be absorbed, come together the only possible result is neurosis in tandem. This applies to friendships as well as to love relationships.

You may wonder why, if this is such a vital aspect of healthy functioning, I have left the discussion of it till so late in the book. It is very simple. *All* of the work you have done until now contains vital information about the limits you have been able to set – and to keep – in your dealings with others. Each of those exercises has been designed to help you reveal yourself to yourself. By now you should have peeled that onion to its very core – and found at its heart your most authentic self. This is the unique self you have created. The challenge for the rest of your life will be to respect that creation, trust its integrity, hold it inviolate from the intrusions of others, and alter it as *you* see fit. If you can do that, you have established boundaries for yourself which will reward you – and those you love – all of your life.

I recently heard a radio interview with Stephen Sondheim in which he said he has spent *forty years* in therapy, learning to say 'no'. Now there's a typical, if extreme, struggle to establish boundaries!

Consider now – just who is this person you see emerging from your work? Is your sense of self-esteem still dependent on the approval of other people? Is your identity still largely derivative, so that you tend to define yourself chiefly through your connections with someone else – as parent, spouse, employee or child? If those primary sources disappeared, would you feel that you yourself had any identity at all? Are you frightened to accept that all human beings are, ultimately, alone? Do you still allow treatment from others which debases or damages or discounts you? Do you continue to give too much of yourself in your relationships because of a fear of being abandoned? Do you allow others to impose their 'shoulds' on you?

Perhaps the person emerging from your pages lives at the other end of the spectrum. Do your essays reveal someone whose tendency is to be way over on some else's side of the line?

Are you aware that your general approach is to try to impose your will, desires and opinions onto others? If those others do not accept your demands, is your reaction likely to be anger, perhaps even contempt? If you can't always get your own way, are you prone to simply walk away from the relationship? Do you use these behaviours to protect yourself from being vulnerable to or engulfed by another person?

Each answer to the above questions will reveal the boundaries you have set for yourself.

This is the last writing assignment you will have. Once again, do not begin this until you have a luxurious, uninterrupted stretch of time to give yourself. You have a lot of assessing and processing to do and you've come much too far not to give it the best of your attention. Pull out your folder now and revel in all the knowledge you've collected about yourself. Read carefully all of your essays, the tattered notes and the jotted observations you've made over these past long weeks and months. Then, and only when you've absorbed every scrap of information, write an assessment of the 'you' your writings reveal in light of the limits you have set for yourself.

As you write, consider how flexible you allow your limits to be, whether they allow room for compromise and manoeuvre. Does that room only include you, or do you grant the others in your life the same space? Can you identify certain relationships in which your borders (or the lack of them) might be causing you difficulty? Notice if you feel that you have established a clear bottom line for yourself – a line beyond which you will not allow yourself to be driven by others' tears or threats or entreaties. Do your writings reveal someone with a keen sense of themselves, a strong awareness of and respect for their own identity? Are you able to recognize your needs and do you devise appropriate ways of getting them met? Do you present yourself to others as you really are, able to express your thoughts and opinions clearly, without undue anxiety as to how they will be accepted? Are you able to give your love freely without fear of being engulfed or abandoned? Are you absolutely clear about the behaviours you will and will not accept from others as they relate to you? Do you believe that you could survive the loss of your most important relationship(s) or your most compelling ambition, still intact, however crushing the pain of that loss? Have you developed the habit of depending on yourself as your first source of strength, stability and reliability? Have you come to believe that you are entitled at least to ask for what you want and have a legitimate need for – and that you are also responsible for your own supply if the one you've asked cannot or will not grant your wish? Have you accepted the hardest truth – that, ultimately, you are responsible for your own happiness and that no one else can give it to you or take it from you?

OK. OK. So you're not *completely* there yet. Who is? Still, that's the direction of your journey. And as someone has said, the journey, not the arrival, matters. Now is your opportunity to take all the time necessary to assess just how far you've progressed along the road.

CHAPTER 18

MOVING ON

*People often say that this or that person has not
yet found himself. But the self is not something
one finds, it is something one creates.*

THOMAS SZASZ

So here we are, back where we started. Has all of the work
you've done through these pages brought you to a new and
richer understanding of the truth of Dr. Szasz's words with
which I started this book? Cast your mind back to the self you
believed you were when you first read them, and consider now
how your growth through these weeks or months may have given
his observation a deeper and uniquely personal meaning for you.
Can you accept now, perhaps in a way you could not then, that
you do have the power to create your life on your own terms, true
to your own developing sense of self? Because that is what this
final chapter is going to address: the future you are going to devise for the self you have thus far created – and the self you would
like to create for the years ahead.

If you've been dealing with the assignments I've suggested,
by now you will have quite a collection of information about

yourself: some of it is bound to please you, some to discomfort you. All normal so far, and a real opportunity to congratulate yourself on the solid work you've done.

But remember that creation is an *active* process. All the fresh insights, and new awarenesses that you've accumulated so far will mean little unless you are prepared to *act* positively in response to them. Think back for a moment to Chapter 8, on acting. Actors may have all the understanding and emotional imagination in the world, but unless they can translate those abilities into action on the stage, they might as well have stayed at home. It is precisely the same for you. So, what are you planning to do with what you've learned? Have you started doing it already?

At the very beginning of this book I also quoted Dr. Szasz in his assertion that 'most clients come into therapy, not to get better but to improve their neuroses'. I have certainly found this to be true. Once the tale is told, almost all clients suddenly find themselves at what the trade calls 'the stuck point', because the relief at finally having been *heard* is enormous, and the telling of the story – your story – usually tremendously difficult.

We are all likely to feel that revealing our deepest truths should be enough; surely we aren't expected to do *more*, are we? Well, yes, I'm afraid so. Unless, that is, we only want to get better at being neurotic.

At this point in my counselling, I have only three responsibilities left to my clients: to listen as they continue to consider what they have learned and are learning about themselves; to help them become aware of and examine the gap which may exist between what they say they want and what they are doing to get what they want; and to challenge them continually to decide what they plan to *do* about it.

My responsibility to you as a reader is to give you precisely the same challenge. And it is one you are entirely capable of meeting – on your own. Even if you have winced away from or even avoided some of the exercises in the book (they will still be there when you feel up to trying them later), since you've stayed with me this far, you must at least be aware of how to set about it. You have developed the habit of writing your life. That is both an enormous accomplishment and an enormous gift – to yourself. As you continue to reinforce this habit in the years to come, all you need to do is to train yourself to examine your writings in the light of two questions for yourself: do my behaviours reflect what I say I want (or believe)? If not, what am I going to do to close that gap – or to solve whatever problem is concerning me?

There is one thing you might want to keep in mind about this problem of 'problems' – and, once again, it is to do with the labelling and mislabelling of things. It is very likely that many of the problems you find yourself struggling with most often are not problems at all: they are facts. A problem implies a possible solution. Facts cannot be solved – they can only be faced. Time and life may alter them, you cannot. But there is a certain peace to be found in simply accepting and dealing with them as best you can, while letting go of the struggle to resolve them. It is that old control fantasy again. Perhaps this is a good moment to remind you of the all encompassing Serenity Prayer: 'God, give me the serenity to accept the things I cannot change, the courage to change the things I can, and the wisdom to know the difference.'

Ironically, I'm encountering the identical dilemma as I write this. I've come so far with you by now – and you have become so real in my imagination – that I find myself feeling the same investment that I do with my own clients. So as I write now, I realize that I'm fighting to come up with some words which can 'make' you take the next, life-altering steps in your own self-scripting. But, of course, there are none. The fact I have to accept is the same one I must acknowledge with every client. This journey is yours, not mine. All I can do is urge you to value yourself enough to continue with your explorations, to act 'as if' when it will benefit you to do so, and to make conscious, creative choices for your behaviours in the light of your new awarenesses. In this instance, the control is entirely yours. I hope so much you will take it.

When I first began this book, I assured you that, if you were willing to undertake the work involved, some slight shift would occur which would allow you to transcend the most severe of your normal neuroses – and live more peacefully with the milder ones. As human beings, a small shift is all we can really ask of ourselves. But remember, it only takes a minor shift in the earth's crust for a major earthquake to take place. It may well be the same for you. But if you do become frustrated with yourself, if you feel yourself too often falling back into the old habits of behaviour and response, repeat to yourself that 'habit is overcome by habit' and, in the meantime, feel comforted by this splendid observation from D.H. Lawrence:

> *Some men must be too spiritual, some must be*
> *too sensual. Some must be too sympathetic,*

> *and some must be too proud. We have no*
> *desire to say what men ought to be. We only*
> *wish to say that there are all kinds of ways of*
> *being, and there is no such thing as human*
> *perfection.*

I need to remind you, too, that psychological insights are road maps to understanding, not immutable truths. So when you find yourself the focus of someone else's psychological bullying, or of too many outside 'shoulds', check with yourself to see whether or not the attitudes and/or behaviours they are spotlighting are damaging to you or to those you most dearly love. If they, in honesty, are not, take a breath, find a smile, and repeat to yourself that there is no such thing as human perfection.

There is a Spanish proverb which says, 'If I am not myself, who will be me?' (When I quoted that to my mother, she said she nearly had to take to her bed on hearing it. She'd never quite realized the extent of her obligation.) I think this observation bears consideration – and makes it all the more necessary for you to liberate that best self which you may be hiding. You know *how* to do it. You know you are *entitled* to do it. So, what are you going to *do* about it?

GROUP
JOURNALLING

*I speak the truth, not so much as I would, but as
much as I dare; and I dare a little the more as I
grow older.*

MONTAIGNE

A suggestion to take with you on your way: why not consider starting your own journal writing workshop? Therapeutic encounter groups can be either dangerous or beneficial, depending on the skills of the facilitator. But journalling workshops can offer similar opportunities for growth and self-exploration without those attendant hazards, and I would encourage you to give some thought to doing at least some of your writing in such a setting. Not, I hasten to say, your most personally revealing writings. But the sharing of ideas which interest and engage you can be a compelling, exciting opportunity for making new or newly profound friendships. My clients have often set up such groups for themselves and I have both participated in and led them myself. In all cases the rewards have been terrific.

If you decide you would like to try something of the kind, it is very simple to do. Sound out eight or ten people you feel comfortable with or would like to know better (they need not necessarily be good friends or even people you know well), and decide on a time and a place to meet. Once or twice a month is plenty. In my experience it's helpful to meet in the same place each time, but if it works better for you to rotate meetings in each other's homes that is fine too, so long as wherever you meet is congenial and free of interruptions. Then at the first meeting you (as the initial leader of the group) will explain that at the end of each meeting the group will be given a topic to write on before you meet again. At each session, every member will have the opportunity to share their writings aloud, if they *choose* to do *so*. There must be no pressure or obligation to read, though I guarantee you that they all will, and sooner rather than later. Your responsibility in this first gathering is to make clear that the purpose of these sessions is absolutely *not* to practise coffee shop psychology by trying to analyse each other's souls through their writings. Reaction is great, psychological analysis is, and will continue to be, forbidden. *The purpose of these workshops is to experiment with using journals or diaries as tools for the sharing and examination of ideas and issues.* The writings will be personal in as much as they will be the reflection of each participant's most honestly held ideas, beliefs and perceptions, but this is not group therapy! And your choice of topics from then on should reflect that intention.

The goal in these workshops is to share your humanness, not to lay bare your psyches. It is vital that all the other participants understand and agree to these parameters from the start. As the individuals become more comfortable with each other, it is almost inevitable that the nature of the essays will become more introspective and revealing. As this happens, it will be your responsibility as leader to see that the sessions remain a safe space for all the members of the group, and to make sure that the emotional temperature is never allowed to get too high. It is fair enough to challenge each other's assumptions, ideas and opinions as revealed in their writings, but these meetings must never become an opportunity to deride or discount any of the *feelings* expressed – or to delve into them more deeply than the writer is comfortable with.

For that first week you will need to have some topic ready for the group to write on (a quotation, a news item, a short poem, one of the suggestions at the beginning of this book – whatever you find interesting but rather emotionally neutral), and then give them 30 minutes to do so. At the end of the 30 minutes, you can either ask for a volunteer to share what they've just written, or you can get things started by reading your own. That first week you might have to encourage some discussion after the readings, but, if you've chosen your group well, that problem will soon resolve itself. *Then* the difficulty will be to let everyone have a chance to be heard. When you're finally ready to call it a day – or an evening – make sure that everyone knows what the assignment for your next gathering is. That's all there is to it.

Of course, the subjects presented for reflection do not have to be limited to the written word. Nor do they all have to be yours. Every member might want to contribute something for consideration. Perhaps someone has been caught by a photograph they've seen, or a cartoon, or a television show. All that's necessary is to provide some catalyst for exploration. The resulting synergy of the group will do the rest.

Below are some possible topics you might find useful for your early sessions as you are getting to feel at home with each other. Later, as your group develops its own unique character, your themes will begin to reflect more specifically the interests and concerns of its members.

1. 'Were we closer to the ground as children or is the grass emptier now?' What resonance does this rather wistful reflection of Alan Bennett have for you? Ease yourself into writing by imagining yourself back into childhood and see where that image of emptier grass leads you.

2. Goethe wrote that 'Manners are morals in disguise.' Do you agree with this statement? As you write about this, try to remember occasions when someone else's 'manners' (or perhaps even your own) might have been used to distance someone, or to make them feel inadequate. What would that have to say about manners – or morals?

3. Pam Houston wrote, 'This is what you learned in college: A man desires the satisfaction of his desire; a woman desires the condition of desiring.' Consider.

4. The word 'hobby' is often used rather apologetically – as if it applied only to unimportant, trivial pursuits. And yet for many of us, our hobbies are the sources of our deepest pleasure, creativity and engagement. Write about your hobbies and their value to you.

5. Identify someone whose biography you could be interested in researching and writing, at least hypothetically. As you think about this, remember that it does not have to be a public person, living or dead. It could be a friend, a relative, a teacher you once had, etc. What is it about this person that intrigues you? What qualities of theirs would you find the most sympathetic? The least? Out of all the people in the world, why would you choose to give your time to this one?

6. If you were an animal (aside for the human one), what would you be? Why?

7. Someone has said wisely, 'It's better to be lonely than to wish you were.' Examine how you feel about this observation.

8. Can you remember the most embarrassed (in-bare-assed) you have ever been? How did you handle it then? How would you handle it now?

9. Write about the location where you spent your most formative years. I do not mean write about the house you lived in, or the family that shaped you. Rather, write about the specific geographical setting that was yours. In what country did you spend those years? Was your place in it urban? Suburban? Rural? By the sea or deep inland? Remote and isolated? Urban and bustling? How important was the physical environment in shaping what you are now? How did you feel about it when you were young? Do you still live there? Would you like to?

10. Imagine yourself (you as you actually are – not some fantasy younger, thinner, better looking, perhaps freer, richer you)

finding yourself suddenly on your own as a tourist in a country other than your own. How would you handle being surrounded by people speaking a language not your own? Would the complete anonymity of such an experience frighten or liberate you? How adaptable do you think you would find yourself to a different culture and different attitudes and ground rules? How would you assess yourself as a representative of your culture? Would your pleasure be significantly lessened by not having someone to share such an experience with? Would it be enhanced? Do your musings about this excite or terrify you?

Once you start structuring these kinds of questions for yourself, you'll realize that the possibilities are limitless. Anything that interests you can become material for your workshops, and choosing a subject for each meeting should soon stop feeling like a task at all and, in fact, become an active pleasure. All that remains, now, is for me to wish for you and the members of your group the same growing sense of excitement and engagement and discovery that so many others have shared in similar settings around the world. Enjoy!

SUGGESTED READING

As I said at the beginning of this book, I think good literature has vastly more to teach about the human heart than all the psychology books combined. That is not to say, however, that there is not real value in many of the works available on this subject. So if you are interested in reading more about psychology – or the keeping of diaries – I am including a list of some of the books which I have found useful or insightful or thought-provoking through the years. This list is sketchy at best, very personal and deplorably incomplete. Of the psychology books I have selected, I have stayed away from the clinical or complexly theoretical. As for the journals and diaries – I have chosen only my particular favourites from an impossibly long catalogue of alternatives. The best I can say about both categories is that they might help you in beginning or continuing your own investigation.

JOURNALS AND JOURNALLING

Auden, W.H. *The Dyers Hand*, 1948.
—— *A Certain World*. Viking, 1970.
Bennett, Alan *Writing Home*. Faber and Faber, 1994.

Bracken, Peg *I Didn't Come Here to Argue*. Harcourt, Brace & World, 1969.

Dillard, Annie *Holy the Firm*. Harper and Row, 1977.

Fitzgerald, F. Scott *The Notebooks of F. Scott Fitzgerald*. Harcourt Brace Jovanovich, 1978.

Frank, Anne *The Diary of a Young Girl*. Doubleday, 1967.

Isherwood, Christopher *The Berlin Diaries*. New Directions, 1963.

Jerome, Jerome K. *Diary of a Pilgrimage*. Alan Sutton Publishing, 1982.

Joyce, James *A Portrait of the Artist As a Young Man*. Viking, 1964.

Mallon, Thomas *A Book of One's Own: People and Their Diaries*. Penguin Books, 1986. If you only read one book on this subject, make it this one!

Pirsig, Robert M. *Zen and the Art of Motorcycle Maintenance*. Vintage, 1991.

Sarton, May *Journal of a Solitude*. Norton, 1977.

Scott-Maxwell, Freida *The Measure of My Days*. Knopf, 1968.

Woolf, Virginia *The Diary of Virginia Woolf*. 5 vols. Harcourt Brace Jovanovich, 1977–.

PSYCHOLOGY

Bray, Adelaide *How to Get Angry Without Feeling Guilty*. Signet, 1976.

Beck, Charlotte Joko *Everyday Zen* Harper Collins, 1989.

de Botton, Alain *How Proust Can Change Your Life*. Picador, 1997.

Dunn, Morrison and Roberts (eds) *Mind Readings: Writers' Journeys Through Mental States*. Minerva Press, 1996.

Kopp, Sheldon *If You Meet the Buddha On the Road, Kill Him.* Bantam Books, 1972.

Lair, Jess *"I Ain't Much, Baby, But I'm All I've Got"*. Doubleday, 1969.

Lerner, Harriet G. *The Dance of Anger*. Harper and Row, 1985.

Lorenz, Konrad *Civilised Man's Eight Deadly Sins*. Harcourt Brace Jovanovich, 1974.

Maslow, Abraham H. *Towards a Psychology of Being Human*. D. Van Norstrand Co., 1962.

May, Rollo *Love and Will*. Norton, 1969.

Millman, Dan *The Life You were Born to Live*. H.J. Kramer, Inc., 1993.

Olson, Paul *The Future of Being Human*. Dell, 1977.

Percy, Walker *Lost in the Cosmos: The Last Self-Help Book*. Pocket Books, 1983.

Perls, Frederick (Fritz) *In and Out of the Garbage Pail*. Bantam Books, 1969.

—— *The Gestalt Approach & Eyewitness to Therapy*. Bantam Books, 1973.

Phillips, Adam *Terrors and Experts*. Faber and Faber, 1995.

Postman, Neil *Crazy Talk, Stupid Talk*. Dell, 1976.

Prather, Hugh *Notes to Myself*. Bantam Books, 1970.

Richo, David *How to Be an Adult*. Paulist Press, 1991.

Shaef, Anne Wilson *When Society Becomes An Addict*. Harper and Row, 1987.

Szasz, Thomas *The Second Sin*. Doubleday, 1973.

—— *The Myth of Mental Illness*. Harper and Row, 1974.

Viorst, Judith *Necessary Losses*. Simon & Schuster, 1986.

Wood, Garth *The Myth of Neurosis*. Harper and Row, 1986.